*The Secret Lore of*
# MUSIC

*Fabre d'Olivet*

TRANSLATED BY
JOSCELYN GODWIN

From the 1928 Edition of Jean Pinasseau

Inner Traditions International
Rochester, Vermont

Inner Traditions International
One Park Street
Rochester, Vermont 05767
www.gotoit.com

First English language edition pubished by Inner Traditions International 1987

Originally published in French under the title *Musique expliquée comme science et comme art et considérée dans ses rapports analogiques avec les mystères religieux, la mythologie ancienne et l'histoire de la terre.*

Translation copyright © 1987, 1997 by Joscelyn Godwin

**Library of Congress Cataloging-in-Publication Data**
Fabre d'Olivet, Antoine, 1767–1825.
    [Musique expliquée comme science et comme art et considérée dans ses rapports analogiques avec les mystères religieux, la mythologie ancienne et l'histoire de la terre.  English]
    The secret lore of music : the hidden power of Orpheus / Fabre d'Olivet; translated by Joscelyn Godwin.
        p.    cm.
    Originally published: Music explained as science and art.
Rochester, Vt.: Inner Traditions, 1987.
    Includes bibliographical references and index.
    ISBN 0-89281-660-0
    1. Music—Philosophy and aesthetics.  2. Music and literature.
3. Music—Religious aspects.  4. Art and music.  I. Title.
ML3849.F213 1997
781'.1—dc21

                                          97-18293
                                            CIP

Printed and bound in the United States

10 9 8 7 6 5 4 3 2 1

Distributed to the book trade in Canada by Publishers Group West (PGW), Toronto, Ontario
Distributed to the book trade in the United Kingdom by Deep Books, London
Distributed to the book trade in Australia by Millennium Books, Newtown, N.S.W.
Distributed to the book trade in New Zealand by Tandem Press, Auckland
Distributed to the book trade in South Africa by Alternative Books, Ferndale

# Contents

# INTRODUCTION
*by Joscelyn Godwin*

This book serves two purposes. One is to share my affection and respect for Fabre d'Olivet, a curious and unique personality whose views on history and cosmology are still worth learning from. The second is to make available the most complete collection possible of Fabre d'Olivet's writings on music. These contain a host of ideas, expressed in nontechnical language, concerning the nature of music and its effects on the human race. There is probably no better introduction to the "Golden Chain of Orpheus," those philosophers who have kept alive the esoteric approach to music from ancient times to our own day, than the work of Fabre d'Olivet.[1] This Introduction therefore serves both as a general overview of Fabre d'Olivet's life and thought and as a more specifically musical biography.

## ROMANTIC MAN OF LETTERS

Our author was born as Antoine Fabre on December 8, 1767, in Ganges, France, a small town near Montpellier in the Languedoc, that region of southern France that takes

---

1. A full account of Fabre d'Olivet's work from the scholarly and musicological point of view can be found in my book *Music and the Occult: French Musical Philosophies, 1750–1950* (Rochester, NY: University of Rochester Press, 1995), which is a revised translation of *L'Esotérisme musical en France, 1750–1950* (Paris: Albin Michel, 1991).

its name from the Provençal language. Until he was ten, Antoine spoke with his mother the *langue d'oc* (the language that uses *oc*, not *oui*, to say "yes"), and he retained a great love for it and for his native soil. His father, a member of a famous Protestant clan, was a manufacturer of silk stockings and a marketer on an international scale. He saw his bright son as a useful adjunct to the family firm and thus packed him off to Paris at the age of eleven or twelve to be properly educated by tutors. Antoine describes this exile touchingly in his memoirs, describing how he spent his nights dreaming of his mother and his homeland.

After five years he returned home, having learned the Latin, Greek, and English languages, and bringing with him his piano. Playing also the violin and cello, he formed an amateur orchestra in his home town, to make what he calls "a detestable music" composed by himself.[2] However, his father could think of nothing but commerce, and in 1786 Antoine was dispatched on his first business trip, back to Paris and then on to various cities of Germany. He seems to have done no business whatever; but he took this opportunity to learn German and also had a strange romantic encounter with a girl called Chrisna, the resonances of which he would feel for years afterward: it would be the subject of his first published song.

Antoine returned to Paris in 1789, supposedly to continue working in the family business, and threw himself into the intellectual and political life of the capital. His sympathies marked him at first as a pro-revolutionary Jacobin, getting his name on a list of undesirables that would later bring him to the unfavorable attention of Napoleon. His talents, at this stage, showed him as an independent *littérateur* who could

2. *Mes Souvenirs* (Nice, 1977), p. 19.

turn his hand to journalism, poetry, and the occasional novel, drama, or opera libretto.

After Antoine found one of his poems mistakenly attributed to the well-known Fabre d'Eglantine, he took his mother's name, d'Olivet, as his surname and discarded Antoine as his first name. The particle "de" suggested aristocracy—an improvement on plain "Anthony Smith," the literal translation of his birth name.

The years succeeding the Revolution saw the ruin of his father's business and of Fabre d'Olivet's hopes for a life of financial independence. In 1799 he took an office job at the War Ministry, where he also placed his father, now sunk very low, as a custodian. We have it on Fabre d'Olivet's own admission that he was able to spend many of his office hours working on his own projects. The first major one, a tribute to the land and language of his youth, was *Le Troubadour* (two volumes, 1803, 1804), a collection of Provençal poetry that is still regarded as a pioneer work of research and revival.

Characteristically, Fabre d'Olivet mixed in with the authentic Troubadour poems a number of pastiches of his own, without distinguishing them as such: the first of several instances in which he combined a scholarly enterprise with an artistic creation of his own and not the only one of his deliberate mystifications.

In the meantime, a decisive event had occurred in his personal life: in 1800 he had met and fallen in love with a brilliant young woman, Julie Marcel, a love which she returned. For one reason or another, however, Fabre d'Olivet was set against marriage, and they parted. In 1802 Julie died, leaving d'Olivet with the agonizing feeling that he might have saved her life if he had not put his principles before love. But several times thereafter she appeared to him, both in dreams and in a vivid waking vision, thereby convincing him of the immortality of the soul and of the presence of a guiding principle—he called it Providence—watching over his life. There is evidence that he later used his wife as a medium to contact Julie. At the end of his life he celebrated her appearance under the name "Egérie Théophanie" at the chief festival of the fraternal order he founded.

## COMPOSER AND MUSIC THEORIST

The year 1804 brought Fabre d'Olivet's well-calculated bid for a musical reputation. He had published the occasional melody in the past, for instance, a silly drinking song (*O Mahomet! tu nous défends de boire un feu divin*, 1793) and tunes for the verses in his novel *Azalaïs et le gentil Aimar* (1799). In the summer of 1804, Fabre d'Olivet introduced an unfamiliar mode in a romance with piano accompaniment, *Souvenirs mélancholiques*, printed by a Parisian publisher, Momigny. D'Olivet called it the "Hellenic mode" because it was a revival of one used in ancient Greece: the diatonic mode on E. He printed his poem (recalling his romance of 1788) and a brief notice of the mode in a journal, *Correspondance des amateurs et professeurs de musique*, August 4, 1804. On the basis of this song, one can credit him with only a very minor gift as a composer.[3]

The next stage of his campaign was a series of six letters on Greek music ("Observation sur la musique des Grecs et sur le mode hellénique qui en est tiré"), which took up nearly half the space of the *Correspondance des amateurs et professeurs de musique* from August 18 to September 5, 1804. These letters show the formation of his views on Greek music that are

3. For the score of the song, see the Appendix to Godwin, *Music and the Occult*.

contained in *The Secret Lore of Music*. Criticisms and counterreplies continued for months.

Readers of the journal were also reminded constantly of Fabre d'Olivet's achievements as a composer, although his only other publication is a lost set of easy quartets: *Trois quatuors faciles et agréables,* Opus 1, for two flutes, viola, and cello. In his letter of October 3 Fabre d'Olivet defends his conviction that the Greeks knew harmony (an idea that would be hotly debated in the succeeding decades) and speaks of how he himself has

> taken the Hymn to Apollo, that authentic piece of Greek music, translated the verses into French so as to preserve as far as possible their rhythm and movement, and after having found a meter that could fit the French prosody, I applied my harmony to the Greek melody. If my ear had been false, the melody would have vanished and I should have made nothing but a musical caricature like that of Monsieur Delaborde when he tried to force the Hymn to Nemesis to crawl among four parts in the major mode. But either my ear deceived me, or the artists who performed this piece flattered me on a vain success, or else this divine melody was by no means displaced, and took on with the modern clothing I had given it all the graces of youth. It was a sunrise that the Greek artists wished to depict, and it was a sunrise that one heard.

Fabre d'Olivet was deceiving himself if he thought that he was resuscitating the moral and emotional significance of the Greek modes, for he attributed to the Dorian mode the scale of C and to the Lydian that of E (his Hellenic mode), whereas the reverse attributions are correct. Consequently, when he thought that he was reflecting the tender qualities of his *Souvenirs mélancholiques* by using the Lydian mode from E' to E, he was actually using the diatonic Dorian mode, which the Greeks regarded as masculine and warlike. In *The Secret Lore of Music* he vacillates between this erroneous scheme and the correct one

(Dorian—E, Phrygian—D, Lydian—C), finally settling on the former. If this proves anything, it is the futility of trying to imitate Greek music while clinging to a modern style.

By December 1804, Fabre d'Olivet was preparing his masterstroke: he had been commissioned[4] by the Consistorial Church of St. Louis du Louvre, the chief Protestant church in Paris, to write an oratorio for their special service in celebration of Napoleon's coronation as emperor.[5] Fabre d'Olivet explains in a later work (*Notions sur le sens de l'ouïe*) why he was forced thus to flatter Napoleon, a man he regarded as his mortal enemy. It speaks well for Fabre d'Olivet's connections in both musical and Protestant circles that he could have his work presented on such an occasion. His biographer Léon Cellier thinks that he may have been feeling his way back to his ancestral faith, after a period of skepticism and deism typical of his time.

On December 22 the great event was announced to take place on Christmas eve, and the new *Oratorio* with words and music by Fabre d'Olivet was to contain several pieces in the Hellenic mode. The conductor of the Oratorio, Rochefort, was *second maître de musique* at the Imperial Academy, and he brought the Academy orchestra with him. Fabre d'Olivet and he were old associates: they had collaborated on a one-act opera *Toulon soumis* with music by Rochefort and libretto by Fabre d'Olivet, performed at the Paris Opéra in 1794.

4. See his *Notions sur le sens de l'ouïe*, 2nd ed. (Montpellier, 1819), p. 15.
5. The manuscript score of his *Oratorio* was discovered in 1978 in the Bibliothèque de l'Histoire du Protestantisme, Rue des Saints Pères, Paris V (see brief article, with a facsimile, by C. Passet and Gilbert Tappa in *Bélisane* 2 [1978], pp. 112–116), but the library in question has been unable to locate it ever since. One hopes that the situation will change some day and enable one to make a proper judgment of Fabre d'Olivet as a composer.

The great day of Fabre d'Olivet the composer came and went, but he refused to let it slip into oblivion. In *Correspondance des amateurs et professeurs de musique*, again, on January 5, 1805, he published verses to congratulate his soloist, Mademoiselle Armand, on her performance in the *Oratorio* of a hymn in the Hellenic mode, and on January 19, he contributed a letter complimenting Rochefort and the orchestra on their performance.

As if this were not enough, an "amateur" wrote a long letter on February 2, berating the reviewer of Fabre d'Olivet's *Oratorio* for having said not a word in praise of its poetry, which he proceeded to rectify with long quotations. Another amateur complains that this is supposed to be a musical, not a poetic journal, and goes on to attack the Hellenic mode again. This gives Fabre d'Olivet the opportunity for his final fling, which he prefaces thus:

> One amateur, two amateurs, three amateurs have written you letters about me by which I am certainly very flattered. Permit me, as a fourth amateur, to join this trio of amateurs, and perhaps we can form an amateur quartet, which won't be as discordant as some I have heard lately....

This concludes the affair of the Hellenic mode, after which the journal itself ceased publication (perhaps because of the boredom that all these letters had caused to the subscribers).

These forgotten panegyrics and polemics show Fabre d'Olivet as the versatile amateur he certainly was, but they also show his egomaniacal streak. He did not have the musical talent to make a professional career— one can see that even from the few measures of the *Oratorio* cited in his last letters. But neither did he have the amateur's sense of proportion, and the result is an excess of self-concern that becomes embarrassing.

Fabre d'Olivet married Marie Warin on March 13, 1805, in

the Consistorial Church then retreated from public life for six years. This was certainly a monumental change of life for one who had formerly vowed himself to celibacy. Marie was only nineteen and continued the education that would gain her a post as proprietor of a private girls' school. During this period she also gave birth to two children, both of whom would distinguish themselves in a minor way: Julie as a painter and Diocles as a historian and novelist.

## Hebrew Student and Healer of Deaf-Mutes

Fabre d'Olivet himself reemerges in 1811 as a full-fledged theosopher.[6] What brought about his conversion? There is no hard evidence for any initiation or membership of esoteric groups, not even Freemasonry. It seems most likely that the change came about through intensive study, meditation, and perhaps mediumistic contact with Julie Marcel. Outwardly it resulted in a large work of scholarship, *La Langue hébraïque restituée,* in which Fabre d'Olivet claimed to have rediscovered the true meaning of the Hebrew language. With this tool, he was able to make an entirely new translation of the first ten books of Genesis, showing them to be a theosophic cosmogony of the profoundest sort, with Moses emerging as the transmitter of this esoteric knowledge from the Ethiopian (!) sanctuaries in which he had been initiated, these in turn preserving the doctrine of divine Unity as it had been held in Atlantis.[7]

Fabre d'Olivet was anxious to publish the work, but the expense was beyond him. His friend the Protestant pastor

6. In current academic writing, "theosopher" and "theosophy" are used to refer to the Western esoteric tradition that concerns the wisdom or understanding of the divine, while "Theosophist" and "Theosophy" refer to the Theosophical Society founded by H. P. Blavatsky in 1875.

7. See *Histoire philosophique du genre humain* (Paris, 1979), vol. I, p. 289 (English translation, p. 193).

Rabaut-Pommier, who had blessed his marriage in 1805, now encouraged him to seek the patronage of Napoleon. The functionary with whom d'Olivet gained an interview seemed sympathetic; when Fabre d'Olivet boasted that he had rediscovered the secret of all the ancient sciences, this functionary promised the book to be as good as published if d'Olivet could prove this just once.

Fabre d'Olivet's lifelong fascination with language, sound, and music perhaps determined the unpredictable form his proof took: the curing of two young men who had been deaf-mutes from birth. Exactly how he did this was never revealed, but the evidence for these and several subsequent cures show that he did indeed have some secret technique that worked in these well-attested cases.

Fabre d'Olivet immediately published a dossier of letters announcing his success, but when they came to the notice of Napoleon, instead of patronizing d'Olivet, Napoleon ordered him to perform no more cures and had him subjected to police interrogation for practicing medicine without a license. Fabre d'Olivet now had no chance of publishing his great book while the emperor remained in power. In Fabre d'Olivet's mind this persecution took on the proportions of a cosmic battle between himself and Napoleon, and it was probably about this time that his vision of the unseen forces behind world history took shape.

There are several interesting theories in the short book, *Notions sur le sens de l'ouïe* (Paris, 1811; enlarged ed., Montpellier, 1819), in which this episode is recounted. The most important idea is his distinction between the faculty of merely hearing, for which Fabre d'Olivet revives the obsolete word *ouïr*, from that of understanding what one hears; in modern French the word *entendre* encompasses both.

Those without knowledge of psychology or philosophy who witnessed d'Olivet's cures were surprised that the young patients did not immediately understand all that was said to them; of course, those cured had to begin learning spoken language like newborn babes.

Rodolphe Grivel, the first, most intelligent, and best documented of all those cured, was able to analyze his sensations, and he felt at first that all sounds issued from within himself. (Having learned to read and write, he was able to keep a diary during the period of cure.) Fabre d'Olivet compares Rodolphe's sensations, and the difficulty he found at first in orienting himself in the audible world, to those of blind people suddenly given sight, to whom everything seems at first right up against their eyes with no perception of depth.

Fabre d'Olivet's analyses and observations show a degree of empathy and imaginative penetration of another person's world that would be rare in any historical period, but were incomprehensible to the medical profession of his time, accustomed as doctors were only to traditional methods and almost medieval ways of thought. D'Olivet speaks thus of the complacency of materialistic science:

> They think they know the world, and do not know themselves; scales in hand, they weigh Saturn and its satellites, and cannot calculate the life of a gnat; they construct systems about the flux and reflux of the ocean tides, and are ignorant of how the sap mounts in the plant; they establish a mechanics of the Universe, and do not perceive the providential laws that are sustaining their own selves.[8]

8. *Notions sur le sens de l'ouïe,* 2nd ed. (Montpellier, 1819), pp. 51f.

## PYTHAGOREAN POET AND ESOTERIC HISTORIAN

Prevented from publishing *La Langue hébraïque restituée* and wounded by the careless and ignorant discussion of his cures in the newspapers, Fabre d'Olivet reoriented his mission. In 1812 the Imperial Institute of France proposed a competition on the theme "The advantages and disadvantages of literary criticism," for which Fabre d'Olivet composed a long essay. His theme was the existence of immutable principles in the arts—of which, however, not everyone was aware—and the necessity of having all literary work judged in the light of these principles by those competent to do so. Such competence is not ascribed to the present arbiters of literary fame, but only to those such as the theocrats of Antiquity—and by implication Fabre d'Olivet himself—who possess higher knowledge of these principles. He presents these thoughts again in Chapters II and III of *The Secret Lore of Music*.

The next year the Institute offered a valuable prize for an essay on the difficulties of introducing Latin and Greek poetic rhythm into French verse, and Fabre d'Olivet again submitted an entry "On the rhythm and prosody of the Ancients and Moderns."

Predictably enough, neither of his entries won the prize, but he had in the meantime made a more public forum for his theories and for his solicitation of the "immortals" of the Institute by publishing his own proof of the possibility of using nonrhymed French verse, in his translation of the *Golden Verses of Pythagoras*. Just as he had sought to introduce the Hellenic mode in music, so now he offered a new poetic resource in what he called *vers eumolpiques*: nonrhyming hexameters in which single masculine and feminine endings alternated. He explained his contribution at length in a "Discourse on the essence and form of poet-ry," which prefaced his book *Les Vers dorés de Pythagore expliqués* (Paris, 1813) and was addressed on the title page to the Classes of French Language and Literature, and of Ancient History and Literature, of the Imperial Institute of France.

*Les Vers dorés de Pythagore expliqués* served yet another purpose, for the Pythagorean verses are used as little more than a pretext for Fabre d'Olivet to produce his most im-portant doctrinal work to date. It is here that he expounds for the first time his system of the three metaphysical pow-ers Providence, Will, and Destiny; his vision of human perfectibility; and his understanding of the transcendent unity of religions. In addition to the books of Moses and the writings of Plato and other Pythagoreans, he notes the following as sources of traditional wisdom:

> The doctrine of Krishna is found especially recorded in the *Bhagavad-Gita*, the one of the Puranas most esteemed by the Brah-mins. One finds that of Zoroaster in the *Zend-Avesta* and in the *Bundahesh*. The Chinese have the *Chun-tzu* of Khung Fu-tzu, his-toric monument erected to the glory of Providence. In the *Poimander* and the *Asclepius* we have the ideas of Thoth. The book of Synesius on Providence contains the dogmas of the Mysteries. Finally one can consult in the course of the *Edda* the sublime dis-course of Odin, entitled *Havamâl*. The basis of all these works is the same.[9]

Fabre d'Olivet barely mentions here the musical aspect of Pythagoreanism, but only because, as he says, he in-tends to speak more about it.[10] One can therefore date the beginnings of the present work to about 1813.

After the fall of Napoleon in 1815, Fabre d'Olivet was at last able to publish *La Langue hébraïque restituée*, largely

9. *Les Vers dorés de Pythagore* (Paris, 1813), p. 233n.
10. Ibid, p. 199n.

thanks to a subscription from the Ministry of the Interior for two hundred copies. The work appeared in two volumes in 1815 and 1816, and was, it is said, better appreciated in England than in France. Perhaps with a definite audience in mind, Fabre d'Olivet had included a literal English translation of the first ten chapters of Genesis that are the substance of the second volume, while the first volume is a Hebrew grammar. Fabre d'Olivet's thesis is, in brief, that the Hebrew of the Mosaic books (the first five books of the Jewish Testament) is pure Egyptian and that Moses had concealed the cosmogony taught in the most ancient sanctuaries behind an outwardly trivial tale. Of course it is still possible to consider the second part of the thesis, even though the work of Champollion and others has invalidated much of the first.

In 1816 Fabre d'Olivet and his family left Paris for a long visit to the Midi, both to see his mother in Ganges for the first time in twenty-five years and to collect material for a revised version of the early Troubadour book. During the years following, he added to his anthology two more volumes, a grammar and a vocabulary of the *langue d'oc*, but they remain in manuscript form to this day. The family returned to Paris in 1817, where the third child, Eudoxie, was born. The next year Fabre d'Olivet went back to the Midi alone to conduct further research.

Offering him hospitality under the pretense of mutual interest in Hebrew, a Protestant pastor benignly tricked him into curing another deaf-mute, the pastor's daughter. Five more cures followed in the area, all but one of which were successful. The renewal of Fabre's therapeutic activity called forth the usual criticisms, which he answered in the second edition of his *Notions sur le sens de l'ouïe*. Again he was harrassed, but not as seriously as in 1811, and now

FABRE D'OLIVET

mainly on the understandable grounds that he refused to reveal his methods to the medical profession. Because of this diversion he did not return to Paris until 1819.

In his absence, Marie, having by then left the girls' school where she worked, had herself written a book on the education of children (*Conseils à une amie sur l'éducation physique et morale des enfants*, Paris, 1820, 2nd ed., 1822), in which she does not bother concealing the signs of marital difficulty. In 1820 Fabre d'Olivet began his most personal document, *Mes Souvenirs*, in which he surveyed the events of his life. In a tragic act of pious vandalism, his daughter Eudoxie censored the manuscript of these memoirs, removing perhaps hundreds of pages to purge Fabre d'Olivet of any suspicion of anti-Christianity, anti-Bonapartism, romantic attachments, and domestic discord. What little is known has been pieced together from other sources, largely through the work of Léon Cellier and Jean Pinasseau.

In March 1821 all three children were baptized at St. Louis du Louvre, an event which Cellier interprets as a victory of the staunch Protestant Marie over her husband's religious peculiarities; while Fabre d'Olivet may have been a friend of pastors, he was no Christian.[11]

He says sadly in a letter of 1822 that his enemies have made even his wife into a rival and a persecutor. Marie left the house with the children, and in March 1823 the separation was made legal. A month later Fabre d'Olivet wrote to the Minister of the Interior to beg support for his work on the *langue d'oc*, saying that he has nothing to live on but a pension of 521 francs per annum from the Minis-

11. This did not prevent him from calling Jesus "a divine man, the most admirable of all those who had appeared on earth" (*Histoire philosophique de genre humain* [1979], vol. II, p. 73n. [English translation, p. 269]), nor from accepting that Jesus had overcome death by a unique act of Will (Ibid., p. 42 [English translation, p. 243]).

try of War. (His salary before his early retirement had been 2400 francs, equivalent to 500 dollars at that time.) He requested a grant of 500 francs such as he had received in the preceding years. Fabre d'Olivet's biographers have no idea what finances the family lived on.

Nevertheless, Fabre d'Olivet's work continued unabated during this period, so that in 1822 he was able to publish another large work in two volumes, *De l'état social de l'homme* (reissued in 1824 with the new title *Histoire philosophique du genre humain*). This is illuminated history on a grand scale, beginning twelve thousand years ago with the appearance of the white race at the Pole[12] and explaining the triple influence of Providence, Will, and Destiny on world events from that time to the present. In Appendix F of *The Secret Lore of Music* is an important passage on music drawn from this work. An idea of its themes is given in this list of fifteen revolutions on which Fabre d'Olivet hangs the thread of his narrative:[13]

1. Appearance of feminine despotism and polygamy.
2. Beginnings of war.
3. Beginnings of slavery.
4. Return to peace.
5. Development of intellect and origin of religion.
6. Political and religious schism caused by the establishment of territorial ownership.
7. Establishment of theocracy.
8. Schism in the Universal Empire on the subject of the sex of the First Cause (see Appendix F).

12. An idea that was much in the air at the time; see J. Godwin, *Arktos: The Polar Myth in Science, Symbolism, and Nazi Survival* (Grand Rapids: Phanes Press, 1993, reprinted Stelle, IL: Adventures Unlimited Press, 1997).

13. This summary from L. Cellier, *Fabre d'Olivet* (Paris, 1953), p. 279n. Fabre d'Olivet numbers only fifteen revolutions, but leads us to believe that there are more after these.

9. Appearance of the political conqueror Ninus.
10. Origin of national representation with the
    Amphictyonic League in Greece (see Chapter IX).
11. Degeneration of religions.
12. Conversion of Constantine and abandonment of Rome.
13. Muhammad.
14. The Crusades.
15. Discovery of the New World.

Some of Fabre d'Olivet's biographers have wondered whether he ever finished the work of which *The Secret Lore of Music* is all that survives. We can say with certainty that he did, for two reasons. First, he is able to cite in his *Histoire philosophique du genre humain* its Book III, chapter 3, and to announce its immediate publication.[14] Second there is a surviving letter dated August 13, 1822, to his former publisher Pleyel, in which he proposes the publication of the work.[15]

In the few years remaining to him, Fabre d'Olivet became involved once again with political figures, in the hope that he might harness the winds of ultramontane Catholicism and royalism for the realization of his theocratic vision. He also returned to literary composition, writing several plays[16] and a translation of Lord Byron's poem *Cain* in which he refuted the author's view of evil.

Most important of all, he founded a fraternal order, which he called "La Vraie Maçonnerie et la Céleste Culture" ("True Masonry and Celestial [Agri-]culture"). A collec-

14. 1979 edition, Vol. I, pp. 185, 246, 250 (English translation, pp. 94, 149, 152).

15. This letter was published in J. B. Weckerlin, *Musiciana: Extraits d'ouvrages rares ou bizarres, anecdotes, lettres, etc., concernant la musique et les musiciens* (Paris: Garnier Frères, 1877), pp. 316f. An English translation is given in Godwin, *Music and the Occult*, pp. 62–63.

16. Only an antislavery play has survived, *Idamore, ou le prince africain*, in *Miscellenea Fabre d'Olivet I* (Nice, 1978).

tion of rules, ceremonies, and Fabre d'Olivet's addresses to the order members[17] tells us virtually all that is known of this order and leaves as many enigmas as it solves. All of its imagery is derived not from architecture, as in Freemasonry, but from agriculture. Here I mention only the musical symbolism to show the significance Fabre d'Olivet attached to the principles expounded in the present book. The following is included for the sake of documentation: it can be understood only in the context of Chapter VII and Appendix E.

In the decoration of the Temple for the first grade of Aspirant, the two Masonic colums are present as follows:

> On the North side, on the right of the Venerable Cultivator, precisely at the point where the white meets the black [wall-hanging], is a column of the Tuscan Order. This column is parti-colored white and black, so that its white part rests against the black hanging and its black against the white. On the shaft of the column on the white side is written in golden yellow the Hebrew word JACHIN, not horizontally but perpendicularly and beginning from the top downwards.... In the capital of the column is traced the number 3. On the base one sees the musical note F, on the G [treble] clef. On the opposite side, that is, to the right of the Typhonic triangle, is a column similar to the one just described. The black of the column is likewise juxtaposed to the white hanging, and the white to the black. On the shaft of this column, on the black side, is written in purple sanguine color the Hebrew word BOHOZ, not horizontally but perpendicularly and beginning from the bottom upwards.... In the capital of the column is traced the number 4. On the base one sees the musical note B, indicated by the F [bass] clef.[18]

In the course of the ritual, "if it is possible to have music, the following Invocation [*Invocation à la Vérité*] is sung,

---

17. *La Vraie Maçonnerie et la Céleste Culture*, ed. Léon Cellier (Lausanne: La Proue, 1973).

18. Ibid., p. 40.

composed in the Solar and Lunar modes called Lydian and Locrian by the Greeks." The ritual for the third and final grade, that of Cultivator, explains further that three sciences study the birth of duality in the Universe: Chemistry, Music, and Number.

> Chemistry [evidently alchemy] is the science of physical Nature, symbolized by the Sphinx. Its study is beset by dangers. Music is the science of intellectual Nature, symbolized by the Pyramid. Its study involves no inconveniences. This is why the founder of our mysteries has engraved its principles on the two limits of the Field, which are the two columns.... At first these two columns offered you the two musical principles B and F engendering the fourth and the fifth by means of the primordial series from 4 to 3 and from 3 to 2.[19]

He goes on to explain that the difference between the fourth and the fifth, the whole tone 9:8, is the emblem of disjunction and dissonance that characterizes the Empire of Typhon, murderer of Osiris, Christ, and all the other suffering saviors, whose reign is now coming to an end.

## FABRE D'OLIVET AS CHILD OF HIS TIME

Fabre d'Olivet died, apparently of apoplexy, on March 27, 1825, having already composed the address he intended to give to his order on Easter Day, April 3. For all his individuality, he belongs to a definite type: what the French call an *illuminé*. He is one of those to whom something has been shown—this much one cannot doubt—something that convinces him that he is the chosen vessel for a revelation to humankind. It may appear as a new dispensation or, as in Fabre d'Olivet's case, as the revival of an ancient wisdom that the human race has lost or forgotten.

19. Ibid., p. 60.

Some illuminates, perhaps the wiser and certainly the humbler ones, keep their knowledge distinct from their personalities. In the same period one could cite Louis-Claude de Saint-Martin as the preeminent example of this type. In others the conviction of their personal mission is too strong for detachment, and then we find the Cagliostros and Mesmers, the Ballanches and Fouriers—and Fabre d'Olivet. Here the sense of self is strong, the sense of persecution nearby, and its materialization in personal disaster frequent.

Fabre was an uneasy child of his troubled epoch. Politically he flowed with the tides to facilitate his all-important work. His religious progress from a Protestant youth through skepticism to theosophic magus has already been mentioned. Although his illuminism placed him in some respects poles apart from the *philosophes*, his possession of esoteric knowledge made him fully as anticlerical as they, and he joined them in regarding his own age as one of enlightenment following a dark period.

Fabre d'Olivet's attitude toward Christianity resembles that of Thomas Taylor, who felt that the new religion added nothing to the wisdom and piety already possessed by Neoplatonists such as Plotinus, Porphyry, and Proclus. D'Olivet regards the Christian religion as an unfortunate necessity imposed by Providence on an ignorant race for their own good! (See Chapter III.) Providence alone, he says, could have foreseen the enlightenment that would follow these unpropitious beginnings, centuries later. And although he looks back to a prehistoric Antiquity in which the gods (he calls them "moral beings") instructed humankind, he expects that golden age to be exceeded by another to come, for which France is a guiding light to all the nations. French esotericists tend to hold the same opinion today.

Fabre d'Olivet's patriotism has the further refinement of favoring his native Midi, the country of the Troubadours who were the source of everything that was good in the Middle Ages. When he speaks (Chapter IIIa) of the Troubadours coming down from the southern mountains to bring civilization to a land so long shrouded in darkness and ignorance, does he not picture himself, centuries later, descending from Ganges to bring another kind of illumination to his own age?

In Fabre d'Olivet's revisioning of the past, all the esoteric schools converge. Chapter VII, "Survey of Celestial Music," opens with a speech by "one of the wise Eumolpids," the hierophants who succeeded in the tradition of Orpheus. The teachings of this personage embody, on one hand, the Pythagorean astronomical system as preserved in the Fragments of Philolaus, with our Earth distinguished from the Counter-Earth "Tartarus," and, on the other, the solar theology of the Emperor Julian, distinguishing the visible from the Intelligible Sun. Whatever its historical warrant, such was evidently Fabre d'Olivet's own cosmology.

In his disdain for the assertions of modern astronomers who base their system on the physical worlds alone, Fabre d'Olivet was in the vanguard of the mistrust of positivist science that has grown so markedly since his day. In the 1620s, perhaps, the Pythagorean revival and the Scientific Revolution could go hand in hand. Two centuries later, and in the face of the Industrial Revolution, it was time for the ancient wisdom to part company with its wayward stepchild. Like Goethe challenging the Newtonian interpretation of color, Fabre d'Olivet speaks from an awareness of other levels of experience, equally authentic, that bring an entirely different attitude to scientific research. His very use of the word *science* is indicative of this: he uses it to mean

THE SECRET LORE OF MUSIC

"knowledge" in the broadest sense, especially knowledge of the "principles" that will always escape the physicalist.

In cosmology these principles are the numerical, geometrical, and harmonic patterns that lie behind the illusory phenomena of the sense-world. Fabre d'Olivet speaks of them (more guardedly than one might wish) in his remarks about the Orphic Egg at the end of Chapter VI, which are probably associated with his concept of "ethereal space." In this space, apparently, the planets hold to their traditional order: Moon, Mercury, Venus, Sun, Mars, Jupiter, Saturn, and it is this order that gives the key of the musical system. A faulty transference of the ethereal order to physical space was responsible, we understand, for the centuries of misguided astronomy between Pythagoras and Copernicus. Yet for the common person, the geocentric universe was a more suitable one to live in, while the complications of different orders corresponding to different levels of being were rightly reserved for initiates.[20]

## Fabre d'Olivet's Place in the Debates of Speculative Music

Fabre d'Olivet is more generous when he explains the principles of music, those "internal and hidden principles" that are grasped not by the ear but by the Intellect, or higher mind. Once these principles are known, as he says in the same chapter, "we can accept them in all certitude and make them the unshakeable basis of our system." Then, and only then, can we hope to recreate the marvelous

[20]This idea would be taken up and devloped not long after Fabre d'Olivet's death by Albert von Thimus. A translation of the relevant passage from Thimus's writings appears in J. Godwin, *Harmony of the Spheres. A Sourcebook of the Pythagorean Tradition in Music* (Rochester, VT: Inner Traditions International, 1991), pp. 371–381.

effects of music known in Antiquity and related by the ancient writers who were, he reminds us in Chapter II, among the wisest and most virtuous people of their time. How dare we dismiss them as frauds; how dare we think that since we cannot obtain any of those physical or psychological effects with our music, that the Ancients could do no better?

As the book proceeds we discover his explanation for their success and our failure. Music is in principle a reflection of the laws of the Universe, but it must be a true reflection if it is to work. In practical terms, this means that it must be true to its numerical principles, those fundamental numbers that govern the tuning of scales and chords. Ever since Antiquity, says Fabre d'Olivet, these numbers have been forgotten or deliberately rejected in favor of some other, artificial system. Consequently we never hear music today that is properly in tune. As he puts it, all we have today is a diatonic system in which only three of the seven notes are in tune, a chromatic system in which every single note is out of tune; and no enharmonic system at all. The Greeks had all three systems, each perfectly in tune with their cosmic principles. No wonder their music had a different effect than ours!

Fabre's argument is part of a long debate on the role of mathematics in music: it is essentially the debate between the Pythagoreans and the Aristoxenians, the former adhering to the primacy of number, the latter favoring the judgment of the ear. Especially since the development of harmony in the West, all our music has been Aristoxenian, because for the chords of harmonized music to sound acceptable it is necessary to make compromises in the overall tuning system. The last and most famous of these compromises was that of equal temperament, forever associated with the name J. S. Bach. Here all the whole tones and semitones are equal (and hence equally out of tune) to facilitate the use of all twenty-four major and minor keys, essential for the fully developed language of tonal music. Fabre d'Olivet dares to doubt whether tonal music is worth the sacrifice: it has not, so far as he can see, improved public morals as the music of the ancient nations was designed to do, nor does it work those miraculous effects on humans and nature that are attributed to Orpheus and even Pythagoras.

Among the theorists who have proposed the restoration of correct tuning, there is a further debate over what correctness entails. The two schools are the Pythagorean, to which Fabre d'Olivet belongs, and the Harmonicists. The Pythagoreans demand that tuning be based only on the numbers of the Tetraktys, the sacred diagram of the Pythagoreans:

.

.    .

.    .    .

.    .    .    .

This series of 1, 2, 3, and 4 allows musical progressions by octaves (1:2, 2:4), fifths (2:3), and fourths (3:4). It is the series used by the Demiurge to make the fabric of the universe, as related by the Pythagorean Timaeus in Plato's dialogue of that name: it is the combined series of the powers of 2 and those of 3, the former giving an endless series of octaves, the latter an endless spiral of fifths that never duplicate a single note. Fabre d'Olivet is a Pythagorean, and this is the tuning that he believes to have been in use among the Egyptians, the Chinese, and every other ancient people.

The trouble with the Pythagorean system is that it cannot produce a pure third, major or minor. As soon as one makes the slightest attempt at harmony, its purity vanishes. Therefore the Harmonicists favor a tuning based as far as possible on the harmonic series, a natural phenomenon perceptible in the higher tones that can be heard accompanying every musical tone. The fourth, fifth, and sixth harmonics make a pure major triad that is the foundation of harmony as we conceive it. The Harmonicists conclude from this that our harmonized music, and its development into a tonal language, is not something artificial, but as firmly based in Nature as the numbers of Pythagorean theory. But their difficulty is that while certain chords can be sounded in perfect harmonic intonation, other chords within the same key, and other keys, suffer as a result. Their solution is either to restrict harmonized music to a very narrow tonal range or to use many more than the standard twelve notes to the octave.

Philosophically, the debate between the Pythagoreans and the Harmonicists is over whether the principles of music should go beyond the numbers of the Tetraktys, 1, 2, 3, 4. In Appendix E Fabre says explicitly that they should not. But they must, as soon as one takes notice of the physical phenomenon of vibration that knows no such limits. The tuning of the pure triad that is clearly audible as the fourth, fifth, and sixth harmonics admits a new prime number, 5, into the system that is not present in the Tetraktys. In traditional arithmology, 5 is the number of Man. Is audible harmony, then, something that begins only with the entry of Man onto the cosmic stage, something that does not inhere in the first metaphysical principles of the universe, adequately expressed by the numbers 1, 2, 3, and 4 alone? And again, should our music stick to metaphysical principles, or should it acknowledge our humanity?

It would be interesting to pursue this debate and the musical theories that reflect it, as it has surfaced from time to time through history: it is by no means dead today. But here it is sufficient merely to mention it, to place Fabre d'Olivet's treatise in its philosophical context.

Joscelyn Godwin
Colgate University
Hamilton, New York

# BIBLIOGRAPHICAL NOTE

All published research on Fabre d'Olivet begins with the magnificent study of Léon Cellier, *Fabre d'Olivet: Contribution à l'Etude des Aspects Religieux du Romantisme* (Paris: Nizet, 1953). Important supplementary sources are Cellier's edition of Fabre d'Olivet's *La Vraie Maçonnerie et la Céleste Culture* (Grenoble: Presses Universitaires de France, 1953, 2nd ed. Lausanne: La Proue, 1973); Fabre d'Olivet's *Mes Souvenirs*, ed. G. Tappa and Cl. Boumendil (Nice: Bélisane, 1977); Gilbert Tappa, ed., *Miscellanea Fabre d'Olivet I* (items I–IV, including the words of the *Oratorio* and the play *Idamore, ou le prince africain* [Nice: Bélisane, 1978, 2nd ed. 1982]); *II* (items V–VIII, including the *Discours sur les advantages et les inconvéniens de la critique littéraire* and the *Dissertation sur le rhythme et la prosodie des anciens et des modernes)* [Nice: Bélisane, 1982]). Fabre d'Olivet's major works are still in print in the original French: *Les Vers dorés de Pythagore, La Langue hébraïque restituée, Histoire philosophique du genre humain, Caïn de Byron traduite...et réfuté.* Most of the articles written about him in this century have appeared in the journals *L'Initiation* and *Le Voile d'Isis* (later *Etudes Traditionnelles).*

Nayán Louise Redfield translated the major works of Fabre d'Olivet into English, published by G. P. Putnam's Sons, New York and London, as follows: *Hermeneutic Interpretation of the Origin of the Social State of Man* (1915),

*The Golden Verses of Pythagoras* (1917), *The Hebraic Tongue Restored* (1921), *Cain* (1923), and *The Healing of Rodolphe Grivel* (1927). Samuel Weiser of New York (later of York Beach, Maine) reissued *The Golden Verses of Pythagoras* in 1975, without the prefatory *Discours sur l'essence et la forme de la poésie* (pp. 1–175 of the Putnam edition), with a biographical note by Ehud C. Sperling, and *The Hebraic Tongue Restored* in 1976. The other English translations have become rare books.

*La Musique expliquée comme science et comme art* was first published as a book, edited by René Philipon, by the review *L'Initiation* (Paris, 1896). This edition was reprinted in the 1970s by La Proue in Lausanne. Clearwater Publishing Company of New York sells the Bibliothèque Nationale's microfiche of the same edition.

Jean Pinasseau's edition of *La Musique...* was published by him in Paris, 1928, and improved on Philipon's edition by containing additional chapters that Pinasseau had discovered. This has unfortunately not been reprinted.

This book contains an English translation of Jean Pinasseau's 1928 edition, checked against the original publication from *La France Musicale*, plus Appendices E and F, and all the footnotes not attributed either to Pinasseau [JP] or to Fabre d'Olivet [FdO] are by the translator.

# PREFACE

## by Jean Pinasseau[1]

The present book comprises: (1) the fifteen articles published in *La France Musicale* under the name of Fabre d'Olivet in 1842, 1843, and 1844, and published incompletely by René Philipon in 1896 (Paris: Chamuel; 2nd edition, Paris: Chacornac, 1910); (2) four articles, under two collective titles: "The Origin of Music" and "Survey of Sacred and Celestial Music," published in the same journal in 1850 without indication of authorship, but certainly extracted from the manuscript that must have been given to the journal in 1842.

In the absence of the original manuscript, the order of chapters is uncertain, and they have been put in what seems the most logical order.

In the Appendix are reproduced: (1) two articles published in the same journal in 1844 and 1852, "Harmony among the Greeks and Romans" and "The Origin of Notation and of Modern Music," which seem attributable to Fabre d'Olivet but were probably adapted by the editors of the journal; (2) two articles, "The Music of the Phoenicians and the Egyptians," taken from *Dictionnaire*

---

1. Jean Pinasseau (died 1972) devoted many years to the study of Fabre d'Olivet. His papers, including some of Fabre d'Olivet's manuscripts, are now in the Bibliotheca Philosophica Hermetica (Bibliotheek J. R. Ritman) in Amsterdam.

*de musique théorique et historique* of Escudier,[2] the director of *La France Musicale.*

Certain repetitions make one think that the original manuscript, which certainly included chapters on the music of the Hindus (see p. 122)[3] and the Phoenicians, perhaps also on that of the Egyptians and the Hebrews, consisted of fragments intended for revision, which would explain why Fabre d'Olivet did not publish the work.

This edition thus only completes the two preceding ones; it is not definitive.

2. Marie and Léon Escudier, founders of *La France Musicale* and publishers of this dictionary, two volumes (Paris, 1844 and several subsequent editions).

3. It seems that the late-nineteenth-century theosopher Saint-Yves d'Alveydre knew Fabre d'Olivet's lost chapter on Hindu music, for he cites it in the manuscript notes for his *L'Archeometre* (Paris, 1912), now in the Bibliotheque de la Sorbonne (Ms 1823, fol. 63). This subject is treated in Joscelyn Godwin's *Music and the Occult: French Musical Philosophies, 1750–1950* (Paris: Albin Michel, 1991).

*The Secret Lore of*
# MUSIC

# I. The Ideas of the Ancients on Music[1]

I AM GOING to examine music in general, as a science and as an art, and try to elicit from this examination a theoretical and practical system based on Nature and uniting the principles discovered by the Ancients with the knowledge acquired by the Moderns.

This study and these results are more important than one might think, for music is not merely, as is imagined today, the art of combining tones or the talent for reproducing them in the way most pleasant to the ear: that is only its practical side from which result the ephemeral forms, more or less brilliant according to the time and place, the taste and the whim of peoples, which make them vary in a thousand different

---

1. Publication is announced thus in *La France Musicale* of 25 September 1842: "Today we begin publication of an unpublished work of Fabre d'Olivet, learned Orientalist and talented musician, who died in Paris in 1825. His heirs have found among the papers of this writer, as original as he is profound, a work entitled: *La Musique expliquée comme science et comme art, et considérée dans ses rapports analogiques avec les mystères religieux, la mythologie ancienne et l'histoire de la terre*. This work, which adds to its ever-fresh observations the charm of its form and the merit of perfect clarity, has been entrusted to us with permission to extract from it everything that might be suitable for the readers of *La France Musicale*." [JP]

ways. Music regarded in its speculative aspect is, as the Ancients defined it, the knowledge of the order of all things, the science of the harmonic relationships of the Universe; it rests on immovable principles which nothing can alter.[2]

When modern scholars read in the works of Antiquity the extravagant praises of music and the marvels there attributed to it, they cannot conceive of them; and since they see nothing, either in the study or the practice of an art which is pretty frivolous in their eyes, to justify these praises or to confirm these miracles, they treat the authors as visionaries or accuse them of imposture, without reflecting that these writers whom they dare thus to insult were the most judicious, wise, learned, and virtuous men of their epoch. Musicians themselves, embarrassed by their inability to explain by way of a modern music which they believe to have attained the last degree of perfection, the astonishing effects attributed to the ancient music, choose to blame its effects sometimes on the novelty of the art, sometimes on the power of the poetry that was united with it, sometimes on what they imagine as the rudeness of ancient peoples. Burette,[3] the least excusable of all because his knowledge should have made him more just, pretends that the marvels told of Greek music do not in any way prove its superiority to our own, and that Orpheus, Demodocus, Phoemius, and Terpander achieved no more

2. Paraphrase of the definition of music in the Hermetic treatise *Asclepius, or The Perfect Sermon*, ch. 13.

3. P. J. Burette, editor of a learnedly annotated French translation of Plutarch's *Dialogue on Music* (Paris, 1735) and of fourteen monographs entitled *La Musique et la danse des anciens*, in *Transactions de l'Académie des Inscriptions*, vols. I–XVII, 1717–1748.

than the worst village fiddle-scraper could do in our time if he could find similar listeners.[4]

This writer, who thus believes that one can assimilate the peoples of Greece to the savage hordes of America, doubtless forgets that, of all the peoples who have appeared on earth, the Greeks were the most sensitive to the beauties of the arts and the most exquisite in their culture. He does not reflect that not long after the epoch in which Orpheus is placed there lived Hesiod and Homer, the most learned of poets; Lycurgus and Zeleucus, the strictest of legislators. He prefers not to notice that Tyrteus and Terpander were almost contemporary with Sappho and Aesop, with Solon and Pindar. I do not know how he would have arranged things in such a contradictory way if he had only reflected on them for a moment; nor how he would have proved to us that those who possessed poetry like Homer's and Sappho's, laws like Lycurgus' and Solon's, sculptures like Phidias', would have gone into ecstasies listening to the music of one of our minstrels; for we, whose music is so perfect in his opinion, who have such magnificent operas, are still far from having anything to compare with the *Iliad* and the *Odyssey*, nothing approaching the Pythian Apollo and the Venus Pudica, although our poets and sculptors keep copying and recopying these admirable models. The brilliant but very superficial author of *Anacharsis*[5] must have worn a very thick blindfold to

4. The same words in *Les Vers dorés de Pythagore*, p. 280 (English translation, p. 75).

5. Abbé J. J. Barthélémy, author of *Voyage du jeune Anacharsis en Grèce*, begun in 1757 but not published until 1788: a popular *Bildungsroman* after the fashion of the Chevalier Ramsay's *Voyages de Cyrus* (1727) that includes much information on Greek philosophy, customs, history, and mu-

have adopted Burette's opinion uncritically; it seems that he ought to have preferred that of Plato, that of Plato's rival Aristotle, that of Plutarch and the judicious Polybius; but to do that he would have had to be in a state to admit the marvels reported by these philosophers, a difficulty with which he dispensed by denying them.

These opinions are nevertheless worth discussing. The historian Polybius, whose accuracy is known, recounts that of all the people of Arcadia the Cynetheans, strangers to music, were regarded as the most savage; and he firmly attributes their ferocity to their having nothing to do with this art.[6] He speaks strongly against a certain ephor who had dared to say that music was only introduced to mankind to seduce and mislead them by a sort of enchantment, and he opposes to this the example of the other Arcadians who, having received from their legislators rules suitable to inspire in them a taste for music, were notable for their gentle habits and their respect for divinity. He draws the most charming picture of the festivals at which the young Arcadians were accustomed from infancy to sing religious hymns in honor of the gods and the national heroes, and adds: "I have reported these things to persuade the Cynetheans to give preference to music, if ever Heaven inspires them with the desire to apply themselves to the arts which humanize peoples; for it is the only way left to rid them of their ancient savagery." Thus Polybius attributes to music the power of modifying behavior. Long before,

sic. The musical portion was published separately in 1777 as *Entretiens sur l'état de la musique grecque au quatrième siècle.*

6. Polybius, IV, 20–21.

Plato had recognized in this art an irresistible influence on the form of government, and had not hesitated
to say that one could make no change in the music
without thereby making a corresponding change in the
constitution of the State.[7] This idea, according to
Plato, was due to Damon, who had given lessons in
harmony to Socrates; but after receiving it himself
from Socrates he developed it much further by his own
studies and meditations. In his works he never lets
slip the opportunity to speak of music and to demonstrate its effects. He assures us at the beginning of his
book on the *Laws* that every part of education is contained in music. "The good man," he says elsewhere,
"is the only excellent musician, because he gives forth
a perfect harmony not with a lyre or other instrument
but with the whole of his life."[8] This philosopher is
careful to avoid what the vulgar were beginning to do
in his time: situating the perfection of music in its
faculty of pleasantly affecting the soul; he assures us,
on the contrary, that nothing is further from right
reason and truth. The beauty of music consists, according to him, in the very beauty of the virtue it
inspires. He thinks that one can recognize the incli-
nations of men by the type of music they like or ad-
mire, and wishes that one could form their taste for
this science early on, by introducing it into the education of children according to a fixed and properly
ordered system. "A State governed by good laws," he
says, "never leaves the basis of musical education to
the caprices of poets and musicians; it regulates these
things as they do in Egypt, where the youth are accus-

7. *Republic*, IV, 424c.
8. The quotation is probably based on *Gorgias*, 482b.

43

tomed to follow what is most perfect, as much in melody as in rhythm and in the form of the mode."[9]

The musical system that Plato had in mind in this passage originated in Egypt; first brought to Greece in its practical part by Orpheus, it was later developed by Pythagoras,[10] who explains its theoretical part openly enough, concealing only the fundamental principle of the science, whose knowledge he reserved for initiates alone, as he had vowed to do in the sanctuaries; for the Egyptian priests did not communicate the principles of the sciences in general except after the most fearful trials and the most solemn oaths to keep silent and not to reveal them except to people worthy of possessing them. Here is the cause of that long silence that Pythagoras enjoined on his disciples, and the origin of those mysterious veils with which he in turn obliged them to cover their teachings.

The musical system that we have today, having come to us from the Greeks via the Romans, is thus in its constitutive principle the same as that of the ancient Egyptians; it has varied only in the practical forms that disfigure it and which one can easily remove, as I propose to show. It is the same system that Timaeus of Locris[11] regarded as instituted by the gods for the perfection of the soul, and in which he saw this celestial music that, directed by philosophy, can easily habituate, persuade, and force the sensual part of the soul to obey the intellectual part, sweeten its irascible part, control its concupiscent part, and prevent these

9. Based on *Laws*, II, 656.

10. Pythagoras' teachings on music are known only through the writings of his pupils and critics.

11. Pythagorean philosopher; the main speaker of Plato's *Timaeus*. See 47c–e of that dialogue.

two from moving contrary to reason or from remaining obdurate when reason commands them.

## France Musicale, 25 September 1842

**Ia.** According to what Plato adds to the passage I have quoted, the Egyptian priests drew diagrams of melody and harmony and had them engraved on tablets exhibited to the public in the temples. No one was permitted to change anything in these models, so that with the same laws controlling all that concerned music, painting, and sculpture, one looked at works of art which had lasted for ten thousand years, and listened to songs that went back to the same epoch. Plato, in mentioning this long period of time and as if suspecting that posterity would doubt its truth, is careful to repeat it: "When I say ten thousand years, it is not just as a manner of speaking, but literally ten thousand years: so one must regard such an institution as a masterpiece of legislation and politics."[12]

The antiquity of this musical system allows one to infer its universality. One also finds it, with different modifications, distributed over all the parts of the earth that are still inhabited by civilized nations, or which once were; Arabia, Persia, all of India, and China have none other. The Arabs, as they themselves confirm, derive their music from the Persians. The Persians have theirs from the Hindus, though they have some difficulty in admitting it; but it is proved by the number and conformity of their modes. All of

12. *Laws*, II, 656d. Also cited in Fabre d'Olivet's *Discours sur les avantages et les inconvéniens de la critique littéraire* (hereafter cited as *Discours*), pp. 12, 18.

these attribute a great power to their music, whose system, which is the same as that of the Egyptians and the Greeks, does not differ essentially from ours except in the deviations of one from the other, and in the external forms that times and places have caused to vary. As for Chinese music, it is basically the same as the Egyptians', as Abbé Roussier has well observed,[13] and consequently is the same as the Greeks', despite the difference in physiognomy it offers at first sight. I will try to explain this difficulty by showing, when the time comes, how it is possible for the Egyptians and the Chinese to have had the same musical system without one of them having given it to the other, but both deriving them from a common source.

In this chapter, so as not to wander too far from my original plan, I will restrict myself to proving that the Chinese have had since time immemorial the same ideas as the Greeks on the moral powers of music.

The famous Khung Fu-tzu, whom our first missionaries in their zeal for latinizing everything called "Confucius," the Socrates of China, after having thoroughly learned music like the wise Athenian, recognized in this science the surest and most agreeable way of reforming public morals and of completely renovating them.

He thought, as Plato expressed it some centuries later, that music should be considered as one of the first elements of education, and that its loss or corruption was the surest sign of the decadence of empires. Khung Fu-tzu was practically contemporary with Pythagoras and the second Zoroaster;[14] without knowing

13. P. J. Roussier, author of *Mémoire sur la musique des anciens* (Paris, 1770).

14. The historical religious reformer, as distinguished from the mythical

46

these divine men, without even having heard of them, he professed the very same doctrine. As profound a moralist as the legislator of the Persians, he had penetrated as deeply as Pythagoras into the principle of the sciences.

The musical system of his country was perfectly familiar to him, and it even seems that he had become quite adept in musical practice. One reads in the *Lun Yü* (Analects) that when this philosopher was playing one day on the *chhing*, a peasant passing his door stopped to listen and, touched by the harmony of the resonant stones of this instrument, exclaimed: "Oh! What great things must occupy the soul of one who plays thus!"[15]

Khung Fu-tzu learned his veneration for music from the sacred books of his nation. These books never speak of this science except to praise it and tell of its marvels.

According to the *Li Chi*, it is the expression and the image of the union of Earth and Heaven; its principles are immutable; it determines the state of all things; it acts directly on the soul and puts man in touch with the celestial spirits. Its principal goal is to regulate the passions. It is music that teaches their mutual duties to fathers and children, to princes and subjects, to husbands and wives. The sage finds in its chords an inexhaustible source of instruction and of pleasure, with invariable rules of conduct.[16] The *Shu Ching*, a

figure; both intertwined in the *Zend-Avesta*, which aroused great interest upon its French translation by A. H. Anquetil du Perron in 1771.

15. *Lun Yü*, XIV, 39; but given a very different interpretation in modern translations.

16. See *Yüeh Chi* (*Yo Ki*; Record of Music), which is part of the *Li Chi*, especially XVII, sect. ii, 11, and sect. iii, 1–2, 28–29.

canonical book of the first order, tells that the emperor
Shun, while naming an official to preside over this
science, said to him: "I charge you to preside over
music: teach it to the sons of the great, that they may
learn to unite justice with mercy, courtesy with grav-
ity, generosity with courage, modesty with contempt
for vain amusements. The verses express the sentiments of the soul, the song puts passion into the
words, the music modulates the song, harmony unites
all the voices and tunes the different instrumental
notes to them; the least sensitive hearts are touched,
and man is united with the spirit."[17] Khwei was the
name of the sage whom the emperor chose to be entrusted with this important task. It is of him that it is
written in the same book, whose antiquity goes back
more than two thousand years before the age in which
the appearance of the Greek Orpheus is placed, that
he knew how to tame the most savage men, to attract
animals and make them thrill with pleasure around
him.[18] It would be too much if I were to cite in detail
all the texts of the Chinese books that speak of music.

Pan Ku, the most famous historian of China, assures
us that the whole doctrine of the *Chings* serves to
prove the necessity of this science. The poets and or-
ators define it as the echo of wisdom, the mistress and
mother of virtue, the messenger of the will of the *Tien*
(the name they give to the Supreme Being), the science
that unveils that ineffable Being and leads men to-
wards it. The writers of all ages attribute to it the
power of making superior spirits descend to earth,
evoking the shades of the Ancestors, inspiring in men

17. *Shu Ching*, Pt. II, Bk. I, sect. 5.
18. *Li Chi*, loc. cit. and also Pt. II, Bk. IV, sect. 2.

the love of virtue, and making them perform their duties. "Do you wish to know," they say, "if a kingdom is well governed, if the morals of its inhabitants are good or bad? Look to the music that is current there."

When one reflects on these ideas which men such as Pythagoras and Khung Fu-tzu alike adopted and which they had their disciples adopt in countries so far apart, after having drawn them from the sacred books of the two most ancient nations of the world, it is difficult to believe them devoid of all foundation and to attribute to chance alone their singular agreement. It seems to me, dspite what a certain Delaborde[19] may say who wrote his four quarto volumes only to prove the superiority of our music, that this superiority is by no means proven, and that it certainly does not appear, as he says, that the Ancients were absolutely ignorant of this art. It is too true that our modern performers, incapable of understanding anything of the marvels of which the Ancients speak, take the part of denial; but a denial is not an answer, and it is not enough to say that a thing is untrue in order to make it so.

It must be proven, and it is impossible to take for an irresistible proof their reasoning as they enclose themselves in the vicious circle suggested by their own egotism. We are very learned in music, they say, and our music is the best of all possible musics; yet all the same we cannot see in it what the Ancients saw in theirs: therefore the Ancients were ignoramuses, visionaries, rustics; and that is that. There is

19. J. B. de La Borde, enthusiastic defender of Abbé Roussier and author of *Essai sur la musique*, 4 vols. (Paris, 1780).

only one point to take up here: it is that one should actually state what is in question.[20]

*France Musicale*, 2 October 1842

# II. THE TRUE CAUSE
## OF THE MORAL EFFECTS OF MUSIC

WITHOUT ATTEMPTING to deny something as well proven as the moral power of music among the Ancients, let us rather try to discover the causes of this power, and lose if we can the bad habit that ignorance and laziness have given us of arrogantly denying whatever is outside the sphere of our knowledge, and of treating as visionaries or impostors those who have seen in the nature of things that which we do not see. Let us try to persuade ourselves that the intellectual vision of man can extend or contract itself, just as his physical vision can; it can penetrate with more or less accuracy and power into the essence of things, just as into space, and embrace in either sphere a greater or lesser number of relationships, according to whether the circumstances are favorable and the opportunity seized; let us recognize that there are considerable differences from person to person and from one race to another; let us take note of times and places, political revolutions and the vicissitudes of nature, and remember that in a thick fog, for example, a man will distinguish objects less well, even though his vision be excellent, than someone with less penetrating eyes who observes them in pure and still air. Thus Europe, long enveloped in a spiritual miasma, has lost the illumination that she received from Africa and Asia; the invasion of the northern hordes has brought upon her all the denseness of the Cimmerian shades. Although her inhabitants are generally endowed with a firm enough moral outlook, and even possess a more penetrating and a much more active spirit of investigation than that of the Asiatic nations, they have nonetheless been unable to acquire the same intellectual knowledge on account of the profound darkness that surrounds them.

The physical sciences, whose torches the Europeans have kindled, have served them well, it is true, to guide them in this long night; but however brilliant their light, they have only been able to show them the external form of things. It is true that they have known this external form far better than the ancient peoples, thanks to these same physical sciences with which need has forced them to light themselves, and which they have brought to a pitch of perfection never attained in any era. One can also be certain that at the moment when the intellectual light, shining on them with all its strength, has dissipated a remainder of the darkness that prejudice, ignorance, and systematic pride still retain, the peoples of modern Europe will see things that could never have been seen either by those of ancient Europe, or by their Asiatic or African instructors.

While waiting for the irresistible course of the universe to bring about this happy moment and carry modern man to the pinnacle of science, let us examine impartially the roads which the Ancients trod, and learn by the waxing rays of intelligence to follow them, that we may eventually surpass them.

Music, whose principles I have undertaken to explain, does not, as I have already said, consist in the external forms: if the forms were everything in this science, I would certainly not write on the subject, for what would my qualifications be? Regarding them as dependent on composition, it would be for the great masters to describe them: for Pergolesi, Gluck, Durante, Leo, Sacchini, Cimarosa, Handel, Haydn, Boccherini. Considering them as intimately tied to performance, the proper people to speak of them would be the celebrated virtuosi: singers such as Balthazar Ferri, Posi, Faustina Bordoni, or instrumentalists such as Zarnowich, Balbâtre, Gavinies, Viotti, Duport. But the forms are transitory things, and less able in this science than in any other to resist the variations of time: scarcely a century passes without three or four compositions which music lovers judged immortal being superseded, destroyed, and buried in their turn. An intelligent composer, an able performer, without knowing in any way the inner principles of these elements, without even investigating them in themselves, but inspired by genius or guided by talent, can fashion these elements according to the rules and the taste of his time, and produce or perform a music which pleases the senses; their success, however brilliant at first, will be brief. Because they have considered only the forms without worrying in the least about the basis they are using, and because their listeners have looked only for pleasure, knowing nothing beyond it, their glory has vanished along with the edifice they have built, while new forms have arisen and met with a welcome by the senses, always friends to novelty.[21] The pleasure which made their triumphs

21. Rameau said: "Music is lost; taste changes at every moment." Marcello had said it before him in Italy, at the very time of Pergolesi and Leo (*Essai sur la Musique*, vol. III, p. 377, and p. 468 of the Supplement). [FdO]

is the cause of their fall: as soon as they begin to bore, they are dead.

It is never by its external forms that music exercises its true power; it is not even by the elements which serve to develop these forms; it is by means of the principles that constitute them. Whenever one imagines that the Ancients caused the marvels which they attributed to music by means of some special melody or harmony, an abstraction made from something else entirely, one is in error. This melody and this harmony were but the physical envelope of a known intellectual principle whose presence awoke in the soul an analogous thought, and by its means produced not only the sensual pleasure dependent on the form but the moral affect dependent on the principle. This moral affect could never fail in its efficacy because the thought that gave it birth connected, through education, to the musical principle, and pleasure itself always followed because the form given by a man of genius recalled the principle and inhered inseparably therein. It was thus that in Egypt one listened with the same pleasure to songs whose origins were lost in the mists of time. Herodotus speaks of a certain song called Linos[22] which had passed from Egypt by way of Phoenicia, Cyprus, and Ionia to the whole of Greece: it is believed to have been the same as the Latins later called Noenia. Plato, as we have seen, has its principle go back more than ten thousand years.

I know well that it is hard enough to understand things so distant from what experience shows us; but let us once more try to believe that we have not attained the zenith of science, and that the sphere of our

22. *Histories*, II, ch. 79.

knowledge is very far from having encircled that of Nature.

Let us cease from turning our strength against ourselves by continuing to deny the existence of that which we do not know. The obstacle most to be feared in the path of wisdom is the belief of knowing what one does not know. Whatever difficulty I foresee in presenting clearly such novel ideas, with nothing to serve me as a thread in passing from the known to the unknown, I will nevertheless try to complete the task I have set myself, and ask the reader to give me the necessary attention.

Music can be envisaged in several ways: by the Moderns it is known merely as theory and practice; by the Ancients it was considered as speculative, intellectual, or celestial. Practical music belongs to the composer or the performer, and does not exceed the limits of art. The man who composes or the performer of compositions receives the musical elements as he finds them, without examining or discussing them; he uses or develops them according to the rules he knows and in conformity with the taste of the people whom he wishes to please, with more or less success according as he is endowed with more or less genius or talent. Theoretical music, besides the composer and the performer to whom it can still belong, also occupies the philosopher who, without himself composing anything or playing any instrument, tries no less to examine with them the elements which they put to work: the musical system as it is used, sound in itself as the result of the sonorous body, and the voice and instruments that modify it. Music thus becomes a sort of science which, inasmuch as it is restricted to the physical sphere, can only be considered as a science of the second order.

It is there, as I have said, that the Moderns have generally stopped; they have scarcely glimpsed the speculative music that the Ancients studied so assiduously and which they regarded, with good reason, as the only kind worthy to be called a science. This part of music served as a kind of link or passage between that which was physical or moral [and the celestial or intellectual kind, and][23] treated in particular the principles as distinct from the forms and elements. But as, following the dogmatic procedure of the Egyptians, no principles of any sciences were unveiled except to initiates and in the secrecy of the sanctuaries, it followed that the principles on which the musical system of the ancient nations rested remained hidden from the profane and were never exposed to the public except under cover of symbols and allegorical veils.

Intellectual and celestial music, finally, was the application of the principles given by speculative music, no longer to the theory or practice of the art pure and simple but to that sublime part of the science which had as its object the contemplation of Nature and the knowledge of the immutable laws of the Universe. Reaching then its highest degree of perfection, it formed a sort of analogical bond between the sensible and the intelligible, and thus afforded a simple means of communication between the two worlds. It was an intellectual language which was applied to metaphysical abstractions and from them made known the harmonic laws, just as algebra, the scientific part of mathematics, is applied by us to physical abstractions and serves to calculate relationships.[24]

23. This insert required by the sense; a line presumably omitted in transcribing the Ms.
24. The same analogy in *Les Vers dorés de Pythagore*, p. 336 (English translation, p. 114).

This, I know is by no means easy to understand in our present state of enlightenment, but we will return to it.

## France Musicale, 23 October 1842

**IIa.**    First of all I must answer the reader who is tempted to interrupt me, saying that if, as I propose, the moral effects of music depend on knowledge of its principles, these effects would be much reduced since I have said that the masses were ignorant of them. This objection is only specious insofar as it is based on modern opinion, and projects our customs and morals onto the ancient nations. In our time the multitude has set itself up as judge of the fine arts. Artisans, simple laborers, wage-slaves, men devoid of intelligence or taste, fill our theaters and decide the fate of music.[25] For a long time a revolution, disastrous to enlightenment and to the development of genius, has given power to the masses and has counted voices instead of weighing them.

The confused cries of a people in tumult, its cheers or its murmurs, have become the rule of beauty. There is not a shop assistant, an attorney's apprentice, an arrogant schoolboy, who following the opinion of Boileau[26] does not think himself more than competent to pronounce on the creations of genius, and who, judging music by how much pleasure it gives him, does not take his disorderly sensations for the measure of perfection in this art.

---

25. Fabre d'Olivet makes the same point with regard to literature in *Discours*, p. 7.

26. "Un clerc pour quinze sols, sans craindre le holà, / Peut aller au parterre attaquer Attila." [FdO] Quoted from Nicolas Boileau-Despréaux, *Satire* IX.

There is not a note-cracker, an orchestral or even a dance-band musician who, consulting an ear guided only by habit and routine, does not presume to be an infallible judge, not only of scales and tones but even of the numbers and accuracy of the intervals admissible in these scales.

This bottomless anarchy did not exist in distant times when music, strong in the simplicity and immutability of its principles, produced the greatest marvels. This science was regarded as so important in China that the government reserved to itself its exclusive direction and prescribed its rules by general decree. It fixed the fundamental note *Kung*, and the dimensions of the pipe which gave it, carved on the public monuments, served as the universal standard of measure. Each dynastic founder took care to create a new music so as to give a new character to his empire. We read in the *Li Chi*, one of the Chinese canonical books, that the music of Emperor Yao was sweet and pleasant; that of Chun made allusion to the virtues of Yao's which it tried to imitate; that of Hsia was grand, noble, and majestic, that of Shang and Chou expressed a masculine virtue, courageous and active.[27] We have seen that in Egypt the laws controlling music were engraved in the temples. Plato, who has preserved for us the memory of this admirable institution, drew from it the proof that it is possible to determine by rules which songs are beautiful by nature, and to order confidently that they be observed. Some centuries before Plato, Pythagoras, imbued with Egyptian doctrines, recommended his disciples to reject the judgment of their ears as liable to error and to variation in matters of harmonic principles. He wanted these

27. *Li Chi*, Bk. XVII, sect. II, 3.

immutable principles to be regulated only by the analogous and proportional harmony of numbers.

It was because of these ideas and the care that the legislators took in maintaining music in its purity that most of the songs were called *nomes*, that is, laws or models. Plato, who lists the different species under the names of hymns, phrenes, paeans, and dithyrambs, does not hesitate to say that the corruption of the Athenians dates from the time when they abandoned these ancient musical laws; for already in his time the masses were agitating violently to have the judgment of music to themselves, and the theater audiences, silent up to then, raised their voices to decide in the last resort the merit of compositions: which made this philosopher quip that the government of Athens was turning from an aristocracy to a theatrocracy.[28]

The poets and musicians, ill-educated in the true goal of this science which is less to flatter the passions of men than to temper them, had given rise to this disorder by wanting to change certain rules that hampered them in their headstrong desires; but punishment soon followed their error, because far from making them free, as they believed, they became the lowest of slaves in submitting to the caprice of a master as fickle in its tastes as the people. Aristotle, though almost always opposed to Plato, dared not contradict him on this point, knowing well that music, once become independent and headstrong to win the support of the masses, had lost it greatest beauties. But this effrontery, loudly condemned by the philosophers, attacked by the satirists, and curbed by the trustees of the laws, was only a deviation from the principles. The pretensions of the people concerning

28. *Laws*, III, 700–701.

59

the fine arts, far from being founded, as in our day, on recognized rights, were only a usurpation caused in the last centuries of Greece by the weakness of the artists, and one from which the latter were well able to extricate themselves when their genius allowed them the means. We know, for example, that when the Athenians wanted to treat Euripides as he had treated many others, and force him to withdraw something from one of his plays to suit their tastes, the poet appeared in the theater and said to the spectators: "I do not write my plays to learn from you, but on the contrary for you to learn from me."[29] It is worth mentioning that at the very moment when the Athenians thus forgot their ancient musical laws and applauded the effeminate accents of the Ionians who, bent beneath the Persian yoke, consoled themselves for the loss of their liberty by abandoning themselves to license, they (the Athenians) were beaten at Aegos-Potamos by those very Spartans whose ephors, rigid observers of ancient customs, had ordered the famous Timotheus to cut four of the strings of his lyre, accusing him of having by his dangerous innovations insulted the majesty of music and tried to corrupt the youth of Sparta.[30]

It was doubtless this event that Plato had in mind when, as I have said, he dated the corruption of Athens from the period when their music became decadent. When they were the victors at Marathon, they still respected the ancient laws, and like the other peoples of Greece watched most carefully over the immuta-

29. Also cited in *Discours*, pp. 7, 19, where Euripides is compared to Rameau. Fabre d'Olivet probably found this anecdote in Barthélémy (see note 5 above), who gives the source as Valerius Maximus, III, 7 (*Les Voyages du jeune Anarcharsis* [Paris, 1839], p. 556).
30. Boethius, *De Institutione musica*, I, 1.

bility of this science; no one was permitted to alter its principles, and the modes, once set up, varied no more; the whistles, the confused roar of the crowd, the clapping and applause were not, said Plato, the rule that decided whether this order had been well observed.[31]

Neither the poet nor the musician had anything to fear or to hope from that. There were in the theater men adept in the knowledge of music who listened in silence until the end and who, holding a laurel branch as symbol of their dignity, pronounced on the works submitted in competition and kept all in order and well-being; thus the Athenians knew that if one is to judge music by the pleasure it gives, the appreciation of this pleasure is granted not to the first comer, but to men who are upright and moreover instructed in the principles of the science, and primarily to one man alone, distinguished above all the rest for his virtue and wisdom.

Thus, then, to return to the point after this long digression, at a time when music was exercising its greatest power whether in Greece, in Egypt, in China, or elsewhere, the masses, far from setting themselves up as judges of it, received it respectfully from the hands of their leaders, revering its laws as the work of their ancestors, and loving it as a product of their fatherland and a gift of their gods; they were ignorant of its constitutive principles, confided to the priesthood and known only to initiates, but these principles acted on them unconsciously and instinctively in the same way as those of politics or religion. It was certainly not the Athenian best equipped to reason about the constitution of the Republic who loved it most and who could best defend it, for Demosthenes was

31. *Laws*, loc. cit.

the first to flee and throw away his shield at the battle of Cheironea.[32] It was not he who knew the divine dogmas in detail who most respected Divinity, for did not Anytus demand Socrates' death by poison?[33] In all countries of the world, the masses are made for feeling and acting, not for judging and knowing; their superiors of every order must judge and know for them, and allow them nothing that would injure them even though it might at first be physically enjoyable. Easily moved and eager to be led, it is from the decision of their superiors that the masses receive their good or bad emotions, their direction toward good or evil. The ancient legislators, who knew these things and understood the influence that music can have, made use of it, as I have said, with an admirable art, an art full of wisdom, but so ignored today that it is only spoken of as a folly fit to be relegated to the land of chimaeras. All the same, this art was not so difficult that it could not be put to use again if one could only rescue musical science from the strange debasement into which it has fallen. I will investigate on another occasion the means that remain to us of restoring part of its brilliance.

*France Musicale*, 30 October 1842

32. The allegation is that of Demosthenes' opponent Aeschines, in the latter's *de Corona*, 65, 13 Neglis.
33. Anytus and Meletus, Socrates' accusers, demanded the death penalty for the crime of "corrupting the youth of Athens by teaching them to believe not in the gods in whom the city believes, but in other new divinities"; Plato, *The Apology of Socrates*, esp. 26b, 36b.

## III. Why the Principles of Music Have Remained Unknown; Vicissitudes of This Science; Origin of the Modern System

If the wise Egyptians and, following their example, those who were instructed by them concealed with such care the principles of the sciences, and if they revealed them only to initiates and in the secrecy of the sanctuary, one should not think that this was because of the obscurity of those principles or the difficulty of understanding them: one would be quite wrong. Most of these principles, and those of music in particular, were extremely simple. But this very simplicity was a dangerous snare which these prudent men wished to avoid. They knew that nothing earns the respect of the masses but that which astonishes or intimidates them, that which is above their comprehension, beyond their powers, or veiled in mysterious darkness. Something that is easily communicated, that shines clear and simple, something that everyone, on seeing it and possessing it for the first time, believes to have always seen and possessed, is degraded in their eyes and they despise it forthwith. One must take care that the truth is not delivered up to their scorn. The masses love error precisely because of the trouble it gives them to create and understand it. They appropriate it by dint of hard work, and that is why they cling to it; they attach a feeling of egotism to their labor, for error is the work of man; and as it is diverse by its very essence, each man may have his own; whereas truth, which emanates from Unity, is common to all and the same for all.

One cannot imagine how many useless and negative efforts men have made since the extinction of the lights and the closing of the ancient sanctuaries to rediscover the forgotten principles of music; how many opposing systems have arisen, conflicted, and fallen in their turn. One would have to have read everything ever written on this subject from Cassiodorus and Boethius up to our own time in order to form a clear idea of it.

The judicious Tartini, after having made a valuable study of those works, avers that he has found nothing to enlighten him even on the diatonic progression of which he presumes, and rightly, that the Ancients deliberately concealed the constitutive principle. "It is quite certain," he says,[34] "that the lack of a perfect understanding of the diatonic genus has always prevented and will always prevent scholars from reaching the source of harmony. . . ."

Those who think that this knowledge consists merely in the study of the musical scale are in error; but their error is involuntary, because how can one hope to penetrate the rationale of this scale? Certainly not by means of the books of experts. There is not a single one that solidly treats this primordial rationale, not even among those that have come down to us from

---

34. Giuseppe Tartini, *Principi dell'Armonia* [Padua, 1767], Preface, p. 1. [FdO]

the Greeks. It is quite true that Pythagoras and Plato have let us glimpse the exterior, in revealing what they judged necessary for the development of harmony which they regard as the immutable law of the Universe; but at the same time they have taken a jealous care in veiling its inner principles, of which they resolved to make a mystery. The later Greek writers such as Didymus, Aristoxenus, Ptolemy, have contented themselves in their turn with casting some light on these outer things that the earlier philosophers had revealed and offered for their discussion, without ever approaching the principles which were not at their disposal.

Roussier,[35] of all the modern writers the one who has approached closest to these principles, attributes to chance alone his fortunate discovery in this regard, considering that nothing of what has been written in recent times could have set him on the way. I will explain later how this learned theorist, because of his lack of method, his haste, and his prejudices, was prevented from reaping from his work the fruit that he should have expected from it, and why a principle as precious as the one he discovered remained fruitless in his hands. First I must forestall a difficulty that may arise in the mind of an attentive reader, by explaining to him the reason why, of so many initiates who must have known the principles of the sciences in general and of music in particular, not one has been tempted to divulge them.

The first founders of the Mysteries, imbued with the principles I have explained and wanting to imitate Divinity, which unveils itself to our senses but likes

35. Roussier, op. cit., pp. iii–iv.

to conceal the mainsprings of Nature, strewed the paths of initiation with difficulties, wrapped themselves in the veils of allegory, and spoke at first only with symbolic voices, so as better to stir the curiosity of men, prompt them to make investigations, and test their constancy in the face of the innumerable trials they made them undergo. Those who attained the final grades of initiation swore never to betray the secrets entrusted to them, and took the most formidable oaths at the altars of Ceres or Isis. They were not permitted to write of them in any fashion, and could speak of them out loud only with initiates. The penalty of death was decreed both to the perjurer who dared to violate his oaths, and to the uninitiated who indiscreetly tried to profane the Mysteries.

Public opinion was so strong in this regard that the criminal, whoever he might be, found no sanctuary, and everyone shunned him with horror. The poet Aeschylus, suspected of having revealed on the stage a subject from the Mysteries, only just escaped the wrath of the people, and could acquit himself of the crime he was accused of only by proving that he had never been initiated. A price was put upon the head of Diagoras for the same reason. Andocides and Alcibiades were accused, and ran the risk of losing their lives. Aristotle himself only just escaped the persecutions of the hierophant Eurymedon. Finally Philolaus ran a great risk, and Aristarchus of Samos was summoned before the law, the first for having said, and the second for having written that the earth is not the center of the universe, thereby divulging a truth that Pythagoras had taught only under the veil of symbols.

Thus those of the initiates whom the sanctity of oaths would not have been strong enough to restrain were prevented from speaking by fear of punishment; and as everything concerning the principles was oral and traditional, it depended entirely on the hierophant, sole depository of the ancient traditions, to measure his revelations against the known capacity of the initiates. Thus he did, so long as the Mysteries preserved their original purity and he himself was worthy of receiving and preserving them; but as soon as the corruption of public morals had corrupted the laws as well, as soon as the sanctuary itself was no longer safe from invasion and the hierophant himself ceased to be the most virtuous of men, then, receiving the tradition without appreciating or comprehending it, he scorned its simplicity and altered it in all sorts of ways so as to match it to his false ideas. Initiation, degenerating imperceptibly, became no more than an empty ceremony. The priests of Ceres, like those of Isis and Cybele, fell into disrepute and through their ridiculous farces and scandalous morals became the laughing-stock of the populace. The secret of the Mysteries disappeared along with the virtue that had been their lifeblood. Patrons such as Commodus, Caracalla, and Domitian, seeking to reanimate this corpse, added further to its corruption, and the Mysteries, now thoroughly degenerated, were no more than schools of debauch, while in Rome the virtuous Isis had in place of a sanctuary nothing but a brothel, known as the Garden of the Goddess.

If a few privileged men in the midst of this chaos grasped at a scrap of the truth floating on the mass of errors and dared to produce it, they were either not understood or, struck by the shafts of ridicule, they fell victim to arrogant ignorance. The opinions and prejudices of the people set themselves up everywhere as science, and those who had talents now used them only to give these illusions some sort of consistency, decking them out with a semblance of reason. It was thus that the celebrated Ptolemy, in the second century of the Christian era, after having through calculation reduced to an astronomical system the popular notion of the motions of the celestial bodies, also undertook to give a foundation to the musical errors of his time.[36] He had been guided in the first enterprise by Eudoxus; in the second by Didymus and Aristoxenus. This Aristoxenus, disciple of Aristotle and consequently an enemy of Plato, had written his book with the sole object of attacking the speculative doctrine, opposing the physical to the moral, the sensible to the intellectual, and thus of raising up the Lyceum on the debris of the Academy. He maintained, against the opinion of Pythagoras, that it was for the ear alone to judge the correctness of musical tunings. One can see from what Cicero reports to what degree he corrupted the ideas of Plato while seeming to explain them. He said that just as when the melody is in the instrument, it is the ratios of the chords that make the harmony, so all the parts of the body are so disposed that from the relations they have to one another, the soul results.

Here is the idea that Cabanis[37] has all too eloquently developed, in presenting, like Aristoxenus, the soul as a faculty of the body. Of the 453 volumes that Aris-

36. Besides formulating in his astronomical works the geocentric system that bears his name, Ptolemy wrote the *Harmonics*, the source of the tuning system most often cited as an alternative to the Pythagorean.

37. P. J. G. Cabanis, physiologist and author of *Rapports du physique et du moral de l'homme*, read to the Institut des Sciences, 1786–87. Also cited in *Notions sur le sens de l'ouïe* (1819), pp. 95f.

toxenus wrote, one alone remains to us: the one on music that Meibom has translated.[38]

## France Musicale, 1 January 1843

**IIIa.**   Theon of Smyrna,[39] a pupil of Plato, wrote to defend his master's doctrine; since he was doubtless an initiate and unable to speak openly of the principles, his comparisons and obscure expressions could not prevent the rapid ascendancy of Aristoxenus' system, seemingly clearer and more closely connected with the physics of Aristotle, whose fame was beginning to be known. Besides, minds strongly inclined toward materialism offered to everything physical a foothold that metaphysics could no longer find there. Thus two rival sects arose: that of the Pythagoreans, who wanted the musical intervals to be fixed according to certain authentic ratios whose principles they would not reveal; and that of the Aristoxenians, who claimed to follow the judgment of the ear for fixing these same intervals, whose ratios they indicated through calculation or experience.

There is no doubt that these two contending sects produced a whole multitude of polemical books from whose vain discussions time has spared us. We know only that Damon the teacher of Socrates, Analixas king of Zancle (Messina), Aristophanes, the famous Democritus of Abdera, Antisthenes the founder of the

38. *Elementa harmonica.* Marcus Meibom made this available in Latin in his *Antiquae musicae auctores septem graecae et latinae* (Amsterdam, 1652). English translation by Henry Stewart Macran, *The Harmonics of Aristoxenus* (Oxford, 1902). The attribution of 453 books to Aristoxenus is from Suidas' *Lexicon.*
39. Author of *Mathematics Useful for Understanding Plato,* English translation by Robert and Deborah Lawlor (San Diego, 1979).

Cynics, Euclid, Diocles, Philolaus, Timotheus, Melan-
ippides, Lucian, Porphyry, Apuleius, Iamblichus, and
a host of others have written on music. We have the
treatise of Plutarch[40] in which one can see that, far
from solving the question, all these disputes had
served only to confuse it further. From forgetfulness
of the principles and the uncertainty of experience
were born a host of contradictions. Everyone had his
own system and his own tuning. Ptolemy, who as I
have said undertook to submit these discordant opinions to certain rules, was obliged to admit five diatonic
systems: the "soft diatonic," the "tonic," the "ancient," the "intense," and the "equal." Finally the
ever-growing darkness was compounded by the sub-
mersion of the Roman Empire which, invaded on the
one side by a religion, ravaged on the other by ever-
renewed swarms of barbarians, devoid of virtue and
consequently unable to resist this double assault, gave
way here and there, tore itself apart, and ended by
burying in its collapse the little science and light that
remained to it.

Music disappeared.[41] The wild hordes that claimed
the empire of the world were constitutionally too
crude and dense to relish the beauties of melody, and
the religion which Providence[42] prepared for them,
born in obscurity and raised among the most ignorant
classes of the people, was by no means destined at first

40. The *De Musica* formerly attributed to Plutarch; English translation
by Andrew Barker in A. Barker, ed., *Greek Musical Writings I: The Musician and his Art* (Cambridge, 1984).
41. A similar passage on the death of poetry is in Fabre d'Olivet's *Dissertation sur le rhythme et la prosodie des anciens et des modernes* (hereafter cited as *Dissertation*), p. 24.
42. Providence, with Will and Destiny, is one of the three powers that
preside over Fabre d'Olivet's universe. Most writers would simply call it
"God": it seeks to lead all things to unity.

to inspire them with love for the sciences. It was a bridle imposed on their barbarity, a ferment necessary for the future renewal of the light. I will not recall here the frightful pictures that contemporary writers have drawn of these devastating hordes. The historian Procopius tells us that humanitarian feeling halted his pen, and that he did not want to transmit to posterity details that would appall them.[43] Idacius, Isidore, Victor of Saint Vitus, Saint Augustine search in vain for expressions strong enough to paint the horrors of which they were the unhappy witnesses. These barbarians were not only ignorant of the arts, they also despised them. The name "Roman" suggested to them all that they could imagine of baseness and cowardice, avarice and vice. They regarded the sciences as the source of the soul's corruption and depravity. Now the first Christians had exactly the same ideas. As all historians concur, they were men of the lowest condition, without education or letters. They condemned all the arts as pernicious, and commerce as iniquitous. One of their most celebrated writers, Clement of Alexandria, proscribed both vocal and instrumental music, especially flute-playing. Thus the people and the law to which they had to submit were made for one another, and Providence alone could foresee that out of this dreadful amalgam would arise the wise and enlightened nation that now dominates Europe, and from whose bosom the sciences shall arise more brilliant than ever.

Plutarch[44] tells that a king of the Scythians called Atheas, having heard an accomplished flute-player,

43. The same passage in *Histoire philosophique du genre humain* (1979), vol. II, p. 61n. (English translation, p. 259n.).

44. In the treatise *That Epicurus actually makes a pleasant life impossible*, in *Moralia*, 1095F.

said that he would rather listen to his horse's whin-
nying. We know from an infinitude of witnesses that
these peoples had such an aversion for the sciences
and for the books that treat of them that they destroyed them wherever war made them masters. Rap-
ine and fire followed in their wake. This spirit of
hatred and destruction was heated and fed still further
by that of an intolerant religion. Nearly three centuries
after their most violent invasion, thus at a time when
they were long settled and should have grown more
peaceable, Pope Gregory nonetheless caused them to
destroy the most beautiful monuments of Rome, and
to burn all the ancient books he could get hold of.[45] It
is to this pope that we owe the first elements of modern music, and the chant that is called Gregorian in
memory of his name. Our melody is still dominated
by this chant, and our harmony was born from it. Saint
Gregory, implacable foe of all that came from the
Greeks and Romans, whom he regarded as inspired by
the Devil, distanced himself as far as he could from
their musical system, and substituted for the ancient
tetrachord a heptachord; that is, in place of the fourth
which for Pythagoras had set the limits of the mode,
this pope used a seventh and required one to sound
seven successive tones in place of four, giving no reason for this change nor basing his musical scale on
any solid principle.[46]

Despite its power and the exhortations of the Ven-
erable Bede,[47] who compares to brute beasts those who

45. For a balanced assessment of Gregory's actions, see F. Homes Dud-
den, *Gregory the Great* (London, 1905), vol. I, pp. 283ff.
46. When he writes of this change in his *Dissertation*, pp. 35f., Fabre
d'Olivet ascribes it to a "religious reason."
47. Reference is to the anonymous treatise *De Musica*, formerly attributed to Bede, included in *Patrologia Latina*, vol. 90.

sing without knowledge of what they are doing, Gregorian music was for a long time unknown in the two Gauls; the barbarian peoples who occupied these lands had too little taste, too little flexibility in their vocal organs, to feel the charms of music or to try to learn this art. Their dull language, filled with guttural sounds, was more apt to paint the croakings of the frogs and ducks who populated the marshes from which they emerged,[48] than the sweet melody of birds who breathed the purer air of the southern mountains. Despite the efforts made successively in France by Pepin, Charlemagne, and Louis the Pious, for a long time church music consisted only of a sort of raucous and monotonous psalmody, into which Saint Ambrose had tried before Saint Gregory's reform to mix some phrases of the ancient chants, some debris salvaged from destruction. King Alfred also made unsuccessful attempts to introduce Gregorian chant into England. Music was unable to emerge from its slumber[49] until a spark of genius pierced the dark night that covered Europe, and from the heights of the Occitanian mountains were seen descending the first modern poets and the first modern singers. It is to the Troubadours that we owe the renaissance of music. It is they, as I have said in a work of my youth,[50] who, appearing among the shades of ignorance and superstition, halted their ravages.

48. The imagery is from the emperor Julian, via J.-J. Rousseau, *Essai sur l'origine des langues*, ch. XIX; also cited in Fabre d'Olivet's *Dissertation*, p. 16.

49. This matter is explained in an altogether different way nowadays, thanks to the work of the Benedictines of Solesmes, allowing one to make a fresh appraisal of the origins, the nature, and the value of the chant known as Gregorian, as well as of its influence in Italy from the first centuries, and in other countries up to the tenth century. [JP]

50. *Le Troubadour: Poésies occitaniques du XIIIe siècle*, 2 vols. (Paris, An XI [1803], An XII [1804]).

They tempered the harshness of feudal customs, brought the people out of their deathly slumber, reanimated their spirits, taught them how to think, and at last brought to birth this dawn of light whose beneficent day now shines upon the nations.

## *France Musicale*, 8 January 1843

**IIIb.**   The reign of the Troubadours lasted about three hundred years, that is, from the middle of the eleventh to the beginning of the fourteenth century.

At about this time, Guido d'Arezzo, having discovered a new method of notating and naming the tones of music, considerably facilitated its study.[51] Nevertheless, it was not at the court of that prince who is regarded as the restorer of letters to France that this art developed with any luster.[52] It was at this epoch that harmony began to be known, and that what we know as counterpoint was born. Until then, music was restricted to a sort of melody that, to tell the truth, was nothing but a mere psalmody sung in a single part, as one can see from the surviving manuscripts of the song collection of the Counts of Champagne and Anjou.[53] Thus this science, which had been com-

51. Guido d'Arezzo, c.995–c.1050, inventor of the staff and of the solfège system.

52. Fabre d'Olivet's chronology in this passage is so loose that one cannot be sure whether he refers to Charlemagne, 771–814, or to Louis VII, 1137–80.

53. One would like to think that Fabre d'Olivet had himself looked at the "Manuscrit du Roi," prepared for Charles of Anjou in the mid-thirteenth century, now Bibliothèque Nationale Ms. fr. 844, which contains songs by Thibault of Champagne and others. However, this is probably one of the many instances — I have counted over twenty — of apparent erudition borrowed from a rich secondary source that Fabre never acknowledges: Guillaume André Villoteau's *Recherches sur l'analogie de la musique avec les arts qui ont pour l'object l'imitation du langage,* 2 vols. (Paris, 1807).

pletely extinct with the Empire, was revived a thousand years later when the fall of the Eastern Empire[54] forced the Greeks to abandon their homeland, overrun by the Turks: one sees the ancient Greek and Latin writers issuing from their tombs, as it were, and coming to complete what the Troubadours had happily begun. The Reformation of Luther at the same time gave a salutary movement to the human spirit; the discovery of America, the invention of printing also mark this memorable epoch of the history of mankind.[55] All contributed, in short, to the increase of enlightenment.

Meanwhile, as practical music was improving and artists were being trained at the court of Henry II, whither the famous Catherine de' Medici had brought the best musicians Italy had to offer, the savants of the time were seeking to establish the theory of this art; they were reading Boethius and Guido d'Arezzo, and sometimes rising as far as Ptolemy, but lost in the mass of distinctions these writers make, they were far from grasping anything able to lead them to the fundamental principles. Roussier nevertheless assures us that a certain Lefèvre d'Etaples composed around the middle of the sixteenth century an elementary work in which he admitted the proportions of Pythagoras, as he had found them listed in Guido d'Arezzo and Boethius.[56] The fact seems to me mere hypothesis, all the more since these authors are very far from expressing anything clearly on this subject. Be that as it may,

54. Constantinople taken by the Turks, 1453.
55. Luther's Ninety-five Theses: 1517; Columbus' landfall in America: 1492; Gutenberg's forty-two-line Bible: 1456. The same innovations cited in *Histoire philosophique du genre humain* (1979), vol. II, p. 200 (English translation, p. 377).
56. Jacques Lefèvre d'Etaples (Jacobus Stapulensis), *Elementa musicalia* (Paris, 1552), cited by Roussier, op. cit., p. 89n.

this work which perhaps contains a few truths remained unknown, whereas the one written shortly
after by Zarlino enjoyed general success and propa-
gated the worst errors.[57]

Zarlino, to whom we owe the theoretical principles
on which our modern system rests, was choirmaster
at Saint Mark's, Venice. One cannot deny that he was
a gifted artist and an erudite theorist; but he lacked
the genius to follow the consequences of a truth, and
the power to stick to it. Although he knew very well
the legitimate proportions that the diatonic, chromatic, and enharmonic tones should follow, and although he admits that they are those given by nature
and by science, by Pythagoras and Plato, he nonetheless creates, after Ptolemy, a series of wrong proportions and false tunings, in order, as he says, to conform
with the progress of counterpoint which requires
them. Thus according to him one cannot make harmony without violating the principles of harmony, nor
form chords without mistuning the voice and instruments. Strangely enough, Salinas,[58] the celebrated
Spanish writer who opposes Zarlino with some pretty
frivolous opinions, rejoins him on this point and
thinks in good faith, as he does, that one must do away
with the accuracy of tones in order to form them into
simultaneous harmony.

Vincenzo Galilei,[59] father of the famous proponent
of the Copernican system, was the only one who dared
oppose the errors of Zarlino; but he could not prevent
them from rapidly overrunning Italy, whence they
were exported to Spain, France, and the rest of Europe.

57. Gioseffo Zarlino, *Istitutioni harmoniche* (Venice, 1558).
58. Francisco de Salinas, author of *De Musica* (Salamanca, 1577).
59. Author of *Dialogo della musica antica e della moderna* (Venice, 1581).

Nearly all the Italian authors who have written on music, even including Martini,[60] have adopted the wrong proportions of this theoretician, while recognizing their falsity. The famous Rameau[61] in France and Martini in Italy have no other goal in their different systems than that of giving a foundation to these principles which they believe to be inseparable from harmony. In Germany Euler[62] has followed them in his writings on music; and the celebrated Descartes, Kircher, d'Alembert, finally J.-J. Rousseau[63] and a host of others whose names are not worth citing after these have based their calculations on nothing else.

Here, then, are the elements of our modern system according to the theory of Zarlino as generally adopted: of the seven diatonic tones, C, D, E, F, G, A, B, three are in tune: C, F, G; one, D, is either in or out of tune depending on whether one considers it as the fifth from G or the sixth from F; and three are completely out of tune: E, A, B.

These seven diatonic tones give fourteen chromatic ones, because each one can be altered with a sharp or a flat. Now these fourteen chromatic tones are all out of tune, without exception. As for the enharmonic tones, they do not exist.

One can see from this exposition, whose proofs were

60. G. B. "Padre" Martini, author of *Storia della musica*, 3 vols. (Bologna, 1757–81), which treats only ancient music.

61. J. P. Rameau, author of *Traité d'harmonie* (Paris, 1726), and many other theoretical works.

62. Leonard Euler, mathematician and author of *Tentamen novae theoriae musicae* (Saint Petersburg, 1739).

63. René Descartes, philosopher and author of *Compendium musicae*, 1618; Athanasius Kircher, Jesuit polymath and author of *Musurgia Universalis*, 2 vols. (Rome, 1650); J. d'Alembert, contributor to the *Encyclopédie*, author of *Eléments de musique théorique et pratique* (Paris, 1779); J.-J. Rousseau, philosopher and contributor of many musical articles to the *Encyclopédie*.

to be found only in the work of Roussier before I gave them myself, that voices, forced by certain instruments (especially those that train them in music, such as the piano, harpsichord, harp, and guitar) to follow false intonations, in turn force the other instruments that accompany them to play the same notes for fear of being out of tune; and the result of this is that our diatonic genus is partly just and partly false, our chromatic genus offers nothing just, and we have no enharmonic genus at all.

One must admit that if, as Zarlino, Salinas, and Martini state and as Rameau believed, it is in order to have harmony that we have adopted such a system, our harmony does not even deserve its name, and one had better give it its Gothic name, counterpoint; one must also admit that our performers have no cause for surprise if their modern music does not produce the miracles of ancient music, because they have dared to stray from the true principles of Nature, and to corrupt the sensitivity of the ear to the point of accustoming this organ to accepting three out of seven diatonic tones out of tune, to never hearing a single chromatic tone in tune, and to total ignorance of the charms of the enharmonic genus. If the Greeks had had a musical system like ours, I would not in the least understand the marvels of which they boasted; for I would see a palpable contradiction between the feebleness of the cause and the strength of the effect. But I can be sure that the elementary and physical part of this system, closely joined to the intellectual and moral part, shared all its rectitude, and that both acting together on the mind and the senses redoubled by their united action their respective impressions. It is true that the extreme accuracy that the ear, accustomed to this standard, demands of tones, makes instrumental play-

ing difficult and permits few of those brilliant passages, those *tours de force* and bold dislocations in
which our performers place their merit; but as an ancient says, cited by Athenaeus, it is not in the height
of the notes nor in their rapidity that the excellence
of the art resides, but in the energetic and rapid manner in which the notes mount to the heights of the
subject.[64]

**France Musicale, 15 January, 1843**

64. The flutist Caphisias, quoted in *Deipnosophistae*, XIV, xxvi, 629. A
literal translation would be much simpler: "Goodness does not consist in
bigness, but bigness consists in good playing."

# IV. THE ORIGIN OF MUSIC

MODERN AUTHORS who have written on music, unconsciously misled by scholastic prejudices and forgetting (or never having known) that the course of history has not always run as it does today, have placed the cradle of music, according to their prejudices, among the Hebrews, the Egyptians, the Phoenicians, or even the Greeks, giving as the inventors of the art Jubal, Osiris, Hermes, Olen, Apollo, or Mercury. All these peoples except the Egyptians are very recent in comparison to the world, where music flourished long before they existed; and all these personages named as its inventors were not men, as one may easily have been persuaded in order to avoid more taxing researches, but metaphysical beings of an intelligible nature from whom these peoples derived the more or less elevated ideas they formed of the musical art. One need only open and consult the annals of any ancient nation and one will see there, without exception, that music, granted to men as a divine favor, was brought from Heaven to earth by some god or supernatural being. In India it is Brahma, or, which is the same thing, his creative power Sarasvati, who gave the principles of this admirable science; and it is Ishvara, one of the persons of the Indian Trinity,[65] who founded the first musical system. In China it is Fu-Hsi and his daughter, sister, or wife Nü-Hwa who furnished the elements of music, subsequently developed by Huang-Ti.[66] The Chaldaeans attributed these same things to their supreme god Belus and to their first legislator Oannes. The Egyptians traced them to Isis and Osiris, and the Thracians, taught by the Phoenicians, named Olen in place of Belus; the Greeks, Apollo or Hermes; the Celts, Bellen, the same as Apollo; and finally the Scandinavians, at the northernmost limits of Europe, said of their Odin or Wotan everything that the other peoples had said of their gods or their first legislators.

Certain Christian authors opposed to this general consensus of the most ancient civilized nations a text which they thought was contained in the Sefer of Moses, the sacred book of the Hebrews, where it is said (according to Saint Jerome's version) that a son of Lamech and his first wife Kedah, called Jubal, was the father of those who sing to the guitar and the organ.[67] It would be impossible to make a worse translation of the Hebrew text. But it was not so much the fault of Saint Jerome as of the hellenized Jews whose illusory translation he was obliged to follow word for word.[68]

---

65. Ishvara is actually the name of the personal aspect of Divinity in Hinduism; the "Trinity" is formed by the impersonal principles Brahma, Vishnu, and Shiva. Fabre d'Olivet's knowledge of Hindu music is based on the publications of Sir William Jones in *Asiatic Researches*, including *On the Musical Modes of the Hindus*, published separately in 1784, which mentions Brahma and Sarasvati in exactly the same terms as found here.

66. Fu-Hsi (earlier known in European sources as "Fo-Hi") and Nü-Hwa are mythical beings, often shown serpent-tailed and holding a square and compass. Huang-Ti is the famous "Yellow Emperor," supposed to have reigned in the twenty-seventh century B.C.E.

67. Genesis 4:19–21.

68. On the Septuagint and Saint Jerome, see *La Langue hébraïque restituée*, Introduction, sect. 3 (English translation, pp. 47ff.).

This translation, commonly called the Septuagint, enjoyed at the same time such favor among the principal doctors of the Christian Church that they regarded it as divine and preferable to the original. They would not have allowed anyone to diverge from it too ostensibly; and even so, for all his care to follow it in the most important points, Saint Jerome had the greatest difficulty in having his Latin translation accepted, and found himself on the brink of persecution on account of some slight changes he had thought necessary to make in the most shocking places.

This is not the place to examine why the hellenized Jews responded so badly to their commission from King Ptolemy of Egypt, in presenting him in bad Greek more a travesty than a translation of their Sefer. It is enough to say here that their consciences, bound by a divine law and by the most solemn oath, forbade them to communicate their sacred Scriptures to the profane.

It is however true to say that in the passage in question, the sense presented by the Septuagint is even worse and further from the original than that of the Vulgate, because Jubal is given there as the father not only of singers but also of players of the psaltery and the guitar. Saint Jerome, in correcting this absurdity, followed the Hebrew paraphrase, but this paraphrase was far from showing him the truth. Since this text has some small importance, I believe I may give it here in its integral form. The reader will perhaps spare me the proofs that I cannot present here without going far beyond the bounds of a simple digression. Here is the exact translation of the original text:

And the name of the brother (of Jabal) was Jubal, he who was the father (the generating principle) of every luminous and lovable conception. (That is, of the sciences in general as well as of the fine arts.)[69]

One can already see a very great difference between my translation and the two versions I have cited, because it is doubtless a very different matter to say of any being that he is the generating principle of the sciences and fine arts in general, than to say in particular that he is the father of singers or players on the psaltery, guitar, or organ. But that would still be nothing unless one could infer an even more noteworthy difference. This essential difference stems from the fact that both in the Septuagint and in the version of Saint Jerome the generating principle of the sciences and fine arts (or if one prefers the literal version, the father of every luminous and lovable conception), Jubal, is represented as a man, son of a father and a mother, existing in the flesh in a certain country at a certain time, and actually playing or singing to the guitar; whereas he is a universal metaphysical being, a cosmogonic personage, to whose influence and inspiration are due the developments of all these lovable and brilliant sciences in general, and in particular those of music, among all men, at all times, and in all nations. Jubal differs in no respect from Anubis, to whom he is associated by the very root of his name, and we are well aware that Anubis is no different from Thoth, from Hermes, from Mercury, considered as the creators of eloquence, poetry, and music, and sharing

69. Fabre d'Olivet's own English translation of Genesis 4:21 in his *La Langue hébraïque restituée* runs as follows: "And-the-name-of-the-brother-of-him was-*Jubal*, (universal effluence, principle of sound, jubilation, thriving) he-who was-the-father (founder) of-every-conception, hint-brightness-like and love-worthy (useful and pleasing arts)."

this prerogative with Osiris, Apollo, and Olen. The father whom Moses gives to Jubal is no more a human being than he: he is a being of the same species as Jubal, a metaphysical being who precedes him in the order of cosmogonic generations. One must say the same about the father of Lamech and of all the other personages who are named before him. If one reads attentively the words that Moses puts into the mouth of this Lamech, even in the Vulgate, one will readily see that they cannot apply to any human being. For where is the man who would say seriously and proudly of himself that because he has killed a man for wounding him, and a young man for bruising him, his death shall be avenged seventy-seven times? It makes no sense.

This error, whose consequences are of the highest importance if one wants to understand the ancient sciences, has its source in the ignorance of most of the erudite Moderns of the way in which the Ancients wrote history. This has no resemblance to our own. The Ancients considered things in general and in their metaphysical relationships. We note dates and facts with scrupulous accuracy; we follow step by step the lives of individuals who did not concern them in the least. Their history, entrusted to human memory or preserved in the priestly archives of the temples in separate fragments of poetry, were all allegorical; individual people were nothing to it; it saw everywhere the universal spirit that moved them, it personified all its faculties, opposed them to one another, and set out to describe their birth, their progress, and their developments. It is in transforming these spiritual faculties, or, if one prefers, these moral beings, into so many human individuals, that we have fallen into such shocking contradictions with regard to Moses, and disfigured the cosmogony of that divine man to the point of making it unrecognizable.

One of the worst of these blunders, after having seen men where there were moral beings, was without doubt that of seeing human years where there were moral revolutions. Consequently, however long one made the lives of these pretended patriarchs, their small number compelled one to attribute to the earth an extremely recent origin. That has put us in opposition not only with the traditions of other peoples but even with the lineaments of age that the powerful hands of time have everywhere impressed upon our globe. Natural history here argues against positive history. Even if the annals of the Chinese did not support those of the Hindus, the Assyrians, and the Egyptians, which all count a throng of centuries before the epoch in which the Jewish scribes have placed the beginning of the world, it would suffice to examine without bias the ancient monuments which the earth still carries on its surface, such as the Pyramids, the Catacombs of the Thebes in Egypt, the Temples of Mahabalipuram, and the Caves of Elephanta in India; or even to examine as physicists the immense ruins that it conceals everywhere in the stupendous depths of its entrails, to be convinced that the six thousand years that these Jews granted to Antiquity are but a day in the long period of its existence.

F. D.
*France Musicale*, 26 May 1850

**IVa.**    Music, therefore, should not be considered as the invention of one man, for there has never been a man on earth capable of inventing a science, and there never will be. No science is invented. It is a gift that

the human[70] spirit makes to humanity by means of
one of its inspirational faculties. Any inspired science
descends in principle, enveloped in its spiritual germ,
unformed and feeble in its first elements but containing in itself all its developments in potentiality. The
first men who receive it have scarcely the dimmest
knowledge of it. Many of them do not perceive it at
all, and die without having known this treasure that
they were nurturing in their bosom. From others, however, it gives out a dim light. Generations succeed each
other while it develops in silence, grows and spreads
in the heart of a nation. Then a few men more fortu-
nately constituted than others distinguish themselves,
and by their success awaken the attention of their
contemporaries. A new career begins. Love of glory, of
honors, of riches, according to the type of science,
inflame the heart and now serve it as vehicle. A noble
emulation impels a thousand rivals, excites them to
surpass one another, and hastens its progress all the
more since it was originally so slow. Finally a man of
genius appears; his searching glance takes in the science in its entirety; he sees in an instant what it has
been, what it is, what it might be. Boldly he takes
possession of it, and uniting in a single sheaf its different branches, he gives them a new form. In his
conquering might he forces the divine inspiration,
hitherto dissipated, to concentrate itself on him alone,
and reflecting it as on a single focused point he eclipses
all that preceded him, enlightens all who come after
him, and leaves his successors no hope but that of
imitation. Such a man possesses the primary inspiration, in whatever genre. He dominates the science, but

70. Pinasseau inserts a query here, perhaps thinking that "divine spirit"
would make better sense.

he has neither created nor invented it. Moreover, when he himself, or the sages among the nations, writes about the science that he has glorified, it is always to the Universal Being, to God himself or to one of his faculties that they attribute its creation and invention.

Such were the ideas of the Ancients. One may also mention, in particular regard to music, that the Hindus, before speaking of the musical system of Bharata, their first legislator, attribute the origin of the science to Brahma and to his creative faculty Sarasvati, in the same manner as the Egyptians name Osiris or Anubis before Thoth; the Greeks, Apollo, Pan, or Mercury before Orpheus; and even today the Chinese rank, in the same context, Fu-Hsi and his daughter Nü-Hwa before Huang-Ti, to whom they attribute their most ancient musical laws. It is thus that the Eastern Christians, notably the Abyssinians, the Syrians, and the Armenians, in naming various saintly people as the inventors of music, always attribute the inspiration of this science to the Holy Spirit.

As for determining precisely the date of the appearance in each race of the famous man who, blessed with a primary inspiration, molded the destiny of the science or gave it its laws, it would be very difficult, especially for those whose epoch goes back more than three or four thousand years: for with the possible exception of China, where they began early on to write what we call the Annals, it is scarcely thirty centuries since men first bethought themselves in the present world of writing positive and chronological history in the way we write it today. Before this epoch history was, as I have said, entirely allegorical, and the priests who wrote it in verse did not trouble with individuals except in relation to the spirit that animated them and used them as collective beings. Thus in ancient Egypt, for example, where all the kings reigned under the same name, they wrote the history of kingship, not that of the king. Each dynasty was like a particular being with its own physiognomy. A musician or a poet who wrote on music or poetry could not have given forth his book under any name but that of Thoth; and this is why they counted, in Manetho's time,[71] more than thirty-six thousand volumes that carried this sacred name. Today, when the merest compiler places with his name on the title page of his book five or six lines of academic and literary titles, one can scarcely believe in such self-abnegation; but such was the custom in those distant times.

Thus it would be a great waste of time to try to fix the date of the appearance of Thoth in Egypt, or of Bharata in India. Those modern savants who have tried to do so, unable to get beyond the narrow limits in which the faulty translation of the Sefer has enclosed them, have fallen into the most palpable errors. But this translation does not at all represent the text, which of course leaves perfect liberty in this regard. If one wished to know the approximate date of this epoch, one should keep to the text of Plato that I have quoted above, in which this philosopher affirms that the musical system which the Egyptian priesthood still followed in his time went back more than ten thousand years; which would give to this system, and consequently to Thoth as its author, an antiquity of more than twelve thousand years. But Bharata was far earlier than Thoth, at least than the one who was the legislator of the Egyptians; for it is quite possible that there existed in an even more ancient period another

71. Manetho: (third century B.C.E.), author of an Egyptian history in Greek, our main source for the earliest dynasties.

Thoth, belonging to a primitive world, who under the name of Boudh, Baoudh, or Vaoudh served as the model for almost all the legislators of the present world. But this is not the place to explain this historical difficulty. It belongs to the general history of the earth, and here I must restrict myself to what concerns music.

I said that the first musical system attributed by the Hindus to Bharata[72] preceded the one that the Egyptians received from Thoth. This is proven by the sacred books of the Brahmins, where the anteriority of *Bharatversh* over *Mestra-Stan*, that is, of India over Egypt, is firmly established. One can read in these books that several successive emigrations have taken place from Asia to Africa, and that it is principally from the bosom of India that Egypt received its first colonists and its laws. The Greek and Latin writers confirm all these traditions by giving the name of Indians to the inhabitants of Africa nearest to Egypt, and, as the judicious Fréret[73] rightly remarks, by confusing Ethiopia with India and the Nile with the Ganges.

**F. D.**
*France Musicale*, 2 June 1850

72. The *Natya Shastra*, treatise on dance and music, considered in its present version to date from the second century C.E.

73. Nicolas Fréret, 1688–1749, Academician and one of the earliest European students of the Chinese language. Fabre d'Olivet often cites him with respect.

# V. ETYMOLOGY OF THE WORD "MUSIC"; NUMBER CONSIDERED AS MUSICAL PRINCIPLE

THE WORD "music" has come to us from the Greek *mousikē* by way of the Latin *musica*. It is formed in Greek from the word *mousa*, the Muse, which comes from the Egyptian, and the Greek ending *ikē*, derived from the Celtic. The Egyptian word *mas* or *mous* actually signifies generation, production, or development outside a principle; that is to say, formal manifestation or the passage to act of that which was in potency. It is composed of the root *āsh*, which characterizes the universal, primordial principle, and the root *mā*, which expresses all that generates, develops, or manifests itself, grows, or takes on an exterior form. *As* signifies in innumerable languages unity, the unique being, God, and *mā* applies to all that is fecund, formative, generative; it actually means "a mother."

Thus the Greek word *mousa* (Muse) has applied since its origin to every development from a principle, to every sphere of activity where the spirit passes from potency to act and clothes itself in a sensible form. In its most limited application, it is a manner of being, as the Latin word *mos* expresses it. The ending *ikē* (*-ique*) indicates that one thing was related to another by similitude, or that it was a dependency or an em-

THE SECRET LORE OF MUSIC

anation of it. One finds this ending in all the Northern European languages, written *ich*, *ig*, [*ic*], or *ick*. It is connected to the Celtic word *aik*, which means equal, and comes from the Egyptian and Hebraic root *āch*, symbol of identity, equality, fraternity.

If after the etymology I have given for the word "music" one can grasp the wider sense that the Egyptians attached to its root and that the Greeks themselves originally attached to it, one will have less difficulty in conceiving of the different meanings under which the latter understood their Muses, and the universal influence they attributed to the science which particularly designated them. One will easily see why they considered all the arts of imitation as appurtenances of music, because, following the meaning of this word, all that serves to exteriorize thought, to render something sensible from an intellectual state, and to make it pass from potency to act by clothing it with appropriate form — all this belonged to it. The Egyptians seem to have counted only three muses: Melete, Mneme, and Aoede,[74] that is to say, she who produces or generates, she who conserves or designates, and she who idealizes and renders comprehensible. The Greeks, in raising their number to nine, distinguished their attributes further. They called them daughters of Zeus and Mnemosyne, that is, of the eternal living being and of the memorative faculty, and named them as follows: Clio, she who celebrates; Melpomene, she who sings of things worthy of memory; Thalia, she who blooms, who seeks agreement; Euterpe, she who enraptures; Terpsichore, she who delights in the dance; Erato, she who loves; Calliope, she who tells of astonishing things; Urania, she who

74. These names from Pausanius, IX, xxix, 2.

contemplates the heavens; Polymnia, she who explains the different arts. The nine Muses acknowledged as their leader Apollo, the universal generator, and sometimes took as their guide Hercules, the lord or master of the Universe.

Since the Moderns have long since detached music as they call it from musical science in general, I will follow their usage in this matter and consider music as that part of the science which, in order to render sensible the intellectual conceptions of man, uses in the exterior world two constitutive elements, sound and time, taking one as matter and the other as regulator of the form which it gives them by means of art. But tone, as a production of the sonorous body, is only audible by the human ear through the vibrations that it communicates to the air, according to certain calculations based on number; it acquires melodic and harmonic properties, that is, it rises and falls, goes from high to low or from low to high, only according to certain proportions equally dependent on number; and the musical rhythm by which the duration of each tone is controlled is measured out in time only according to certain laws of motion which again depend on number; consequently one finds number everywhere inherent in the elements of music, and evidently anterior and necessary to them, since they do not exist without it and cannot move except through it. Now something that is inherent, anterior, and always necessary to another thing declares itself irresistibly the principle of the latter.

Number is thus the principle of music, and with the aid of its known properties we can discover those of sound and of time in relation to this science. Leaving to physics and metaphysics that which concerns their particular or absolute essence, all that we need to know of tone in itself is that it is distinguished from noise by certain ratios that are again born from number, since, as I have said in another work,[75] noises are in effect only the sum of a multitude of different sounds becoming audible simultaneously, and in a way contradicting one another's waves; and tones are distinct from noises and become more and more harmonious in nature in proportion as the body that produces them is more elastic, more homogeneous, formed from a substance whose degree of purity and cohesion is more perfect and more uniform; so one may conclude that a body is more noisy as it divides more into unequal masses of solidity and texture, and more sonorous as it approaches closer to homogeneity.

From the experiences cited in the work in which I made this statement,[76] it results that the ear of man is opened first to noise, and that passing insensibly from the enharmonic to the harmonic, or from diversity to unity, it arrives at tone. Such seems always to be the course of Nature. *Absolute* unity is its goal; diversity its point of departure; relative unity its way of repose. The physicists who have calculated the number of vibrations which sounding bodies make in a given time, assert that the lowest sound our ears are capable of hearing is that of a body that vibrates twenty times a second, and the highest that of a body whose rate of vibrations attains forty thousand in the same period.[77]

*France Musicale*, 5 **February 1843.**

75. *Notions sur le sens de l'ouïe* (Paris, 1811; enlarged ed., Montpellier, 1819).

76. He refers to the healing of the deaf-mute Rodolphe Grivel, described in *Notions sur le sens de l'ouïe*. These observations are taken directly from that work, 1819 edition, pp. 81f.

77. The same figures are cited, with Euler as source, in op. cit., p. 82.

# VI. Survey of Sacred Music

THE NUMBER 12, formed from the ternary and the quaternary, is the symbol of the Universe and the measure of tone. In expressing myself thus, I simply speak as the interpreter of the ancient philosophers and the modern theosophers, and say openly what the hierophant of Eleusis and of Thebes confided only to initiates in the secrecy of the sanctuary. What is more, it is by no means merely an opinion maintained by a single people, at a certain time, in a particular country of the earth; it is a scientific and sacred dogma accepted in all ages and among all nations from the north of Europe to the most eastern parts of Asia. Pythagoras, Timaeus of Locris, Plato, in giving the dodecahedron as symbol for the Universe,[78] were expounding the ideas of the Egyptians, the Chaldaeans, and the Greeks. These peoples had long since attributed the government of Nature to twelve principal gods. The Persians followed in this regard the doctrine of the Chaldaeans, and the Romans adopted that of the Greeks. Even at the extremities of Europe, the Scandinavians, in ad-

---

78. *Timaeus*, 55c; Timaeus of Locri, *On the Nature of the World and the Soul*, sect. 35; translation by Thomas H. Tobin (Chico, Calif., 1985).

mitting the duodecimal division, also counted twelve rulers of the Universe whom they named the Ases. When Mani[79] wished to take over the Christian religion in order to allegorize it and to call a halt to its still uncertain forms, he did not fail to apply the dodecahedron to the Universe, recalling the supreme Governors of the Ancients which it represented, filling the immensity with a celestial harmony and strewing flowers and eternal perfumes before the Father. It is not long since a German theosopher, a shoemaker named Boehme, a man of extraordinary genius but lacking in erudition and intellectual culture, examining on its basis elemental Nature and the system of the Universe, was compelled as by irresistible instinct to take the zodiacal number as constituting the regimen of the world.[80] He did more: he saw in this number what I do not think anyone had seen since the extinction of the Mysteries of Antiquity: a double rulership, celestial and terrestrial; one spiritual, intelligible, and ascending, the other creaturely, sensible, and descending.

The institution of the Zodiac is due to the application of the number 12 to the highest sphere. This institution, according to a learned modern astronomer,[81] was not unknown to any of the world's peoples. The ancient temples, considered as images of the Universe in which ruled the immutable Being to whom they were dedicated, all bore the same number and the same division. The Peruvian architects had ideas

79. Founder of Manichaeism, mid-third century.
80. It is surprising that Fabre d'Olivet does not cite Jakob Boehme on the Septenary, which is far more important to his theosophy. He refers to Boehme in almost identical terms, quoting from the *Aurora*, in *Les Vers dorés de Pythagore*, p. 360 (English translation, p. 131).
81. Presumably J. S. Bailly, author of *Histoire de l'astronomie ancienne* (Paris, 1775).

in this regard no different from those of the Egyptians, the Persians, the Romans, and even the Hebrews. The number 12, thus applied to the Universe and to all that represented it, was always the harmonic manifestation of the natural principles 1 and 2, and the mode under which their elements were coordinated. It was at the same time the symbol of the coordination of tones, and as such applied to the Lyre of Hermes. Boethius speaks of it in clear enough terms,[82] and Roussier has interpreted his opinions very well.

After the number 12, product of the multiplication of 3 and 4, the most generally revered number was the number 7, formed from the sum of 3 and 4. It was considered in the sanctuaries of Thebes and Eleusis as the symbol of the Soul of the World unfolding itself in the bosom of the Universe and giving life to it. Macrobius, who has transmitted many ancient mysteries to us, tells that this soul, distributed among the seven spheres of the world which it moves and animates and from which it produces the harmonic tones, was designated emblematically by the number 7, or figuratively by the seven-holed flute placed in the hands of Pan, the God of the Universe.[83] This number, revered by all peoples, was specially consecrated to the God of Light. The emperor Julian speaks enigmatically of the god with seven rays, knowledge of whom is not given to everyone.[84] The Brahmins taught, again, that the Sun is composed of seven rays; their sacred books represent its genius, Surya, riding a chariot yoked to

---

82. Boethius, *De Institutione Musica*, I, 20; Roussier, op. cit., pp. 11ff.
83. *Saturnalia*, I, 21–22.
84. Julian in his *Oration to the Sovereign Sun* does not actually mention seven rays; however, Thomas Taylor, in his translation of the work (London, 1793), prefaces it with a poem of his own in which the Sun is addressed as "All-beauteous, *seven-rayed*, supermundane god!" (his italics).

seven horses. The ancient Egyptians, in place of a chariot, imagined a boat steered by seven genii; and Mar-
tianus Capella, who acts as their interpreter, places
the Sun god in the middle of this boat, holding in his
hands seven spheres, which like so many concave mir-
rors reflect the light which he pours out in great
waves.[85] The Chinese scholars meditated much on the
number 7. Like the Pythagoreans, they attributed profound ideas to it. One of their sacred books, the *Liu-
Tzu*,[86] says that it is a number of overwhelming wonder. Finally, even the first Christians, although in
everything they distanced themselves from ancient
ideas, nonetheless divided into seven gifts the influence of the Holy Spirit which is hymned in the Cath-
olic churches.[87] Quite recently a Christian theosopher,[88] examining the properties of the number 7,
taught with great conceptual force, though otherwise
he was unlearned, that there can be no spiritual movement that is not septenary, because this is the number
of the provinces of the Spirit; and because force and
resistance, which are the universal pivot of every action, are themselves the two constitutive bases to
which the septenary number owes its existence.

It is, I believe, unnecessary to multiply citations to
prove the unanimous agreement of peoples on the recognized influence of the numbers 7 and 12, productions of the numbers 3 and 4 by simple addition or by
multiplication. Now I will continue my dogmatic syn-
thesis.

85. *The Marriage of Philology with Mercury*, II, 183–84.
86. The *Liu-Tzu*, by Liu Chou (sixth century C.E.), included in the *Tao Tsang* (Taoist Patrology).
87. "Tu septiformis munere," from the Whitsunday hymn *Veni Creator Spiritus*.
88. This refers to Louis-Claude de Saint-Martin, in particular to the chapter on music in his *L'Esprit des choses* (Paris, 1800), vol. I, pp. 170ff.

The fundamental principles B and F, developing in
inverse directions either by fourths or fifths, that is,
proceeding from 4 to 3 or from 3 to 2, produce two
identical sets of tones.[89] It is this identity that constitutes the musical septenary, and which causes these
notes to be called *diatonic* to distinguish them from
all the other tones that can still be born from the two
fundamental principles, but which no longer resemble
each other, going outside the diatonic order to enter
the chromatic and enharmonic ones. The diatonic septenary of music, born from the union of the two principles, is applied in celestial harmony to the planetary
septenary (though they did not infer from this in the
sanctuaries that there are only seven primitive planets,
identical and really influential in our zodiacal system,
the others being only secondary like the chromatic
and enharmonic tones in our system). The fundamental tone B represents Saturn, the furthest from the Sun
of the primordial planets. The fundamental tone F
represents Venus, the closest of these to the Sun.[90]
The first has a rising motion by fourths, the second a
descending motion by fifths as follows:

89. Starting on any note B and rising by successive fourths, obtained on
the monochord by shortening the string by a quarter of its length each
time (4:3), one finds the series B, E, A, D, G, C, F, B flat, E flat, etc. Starting
on the note F and rising by successive fifths, obtained by shortening the
string by a third of its length each time (3:2), one finds the series F, C, G,
D, A, E, B, F sharp, C sharp, etc. Only the first seven tones of each series
are identical; these form the diatonic scale. Appendix E contains a useful
supplementary explanation of this.

90. It is important to observe that the Ancients called "Venus" or "Juno"
the planet that we nowadays call Mercury; and "Mercury," "Hermes," or
"Stilbon" the resplendent, the one we now call Venus. It is a change of
name made at the epoch when vulgar opinions took the upper hand over
philosophical ones. It is indifferent in itself, but one must be aware of it
in order to understand several passages in ancient writings. Thus when I
say "Venus," I mean the planet [now] called Mercury, and when I say
"Mercury," I mean the one called Venus. In ordinary astronomy one can
keep the accepted names, but in musical astronomy this is impossible and
one must reinstate the true names. [FdO]

| Saturn | Sun | Moon | Mars | Mercury | Jupiter | Venus |
|--------|-----|------|------|---------|---------|-------|
| B | E | A | D | G | C | F |

This planetary septenary, moving in the universal dodecahedron represented by the radical number 12, is its perfect measure, and constitutes the diatonic order of tones and of the musical modes that follow from it. I will represent the image of this motion after having made some preliminary observations.

The first is that a string measured off in quarters to give the fourths B, E, A, D, G, C, F, cannot at the same time be measured in thirds to give the fifths F, C, G, D, A, E, B; hence two strings are needed to represent the two principles B and F.

The second observation is that these two strings, supposing them otherwise to be equal, will be unequal in length, since the F proceeding by fifths needs a greater distance to reach the B than the B needs in order to reach F by means of fourths.[91]

Consequently, and this is the third and most important observation, supposing that these two strings are bent in an arc to represent the universal sphere, and applying to them the zodiacal measure 12, the two hemispheres will be far from equal, although they give respectively identical tones, because the two strings, incommensurable with one another, enclose areas or spaces which, though one cannot measure one by the other nor ever express them in physical numbers, will nevertheless be in the relationship of the musical fourth to the fifth. This will serve to prove that the Universe is by no means contained, as the vulgar seem to think, in a perfect circle, but in a sort of oval, which

91. The F series reaches B after three and a half octaves; the B series reaches F after two and a half.

the Orphics rightly depicted in the form of an egg, and
that the individual spheres of the planets, conforming
to those of the Universe, are not exactly circular but
describe a more or less elongated ellipse, according to
the portion of the harmonic string that serves them as
measure.[92]

**F.D.**
***France Musicale*, 9 June 1850**

92. This passage would have pleased Johannes Kepler, the original dis-
coverer of the planets' elliptical orbits and proposer of the music made
thereby (see his *Harmonices Mundi* [Linz, 1619]). The parallel with the
World-Egg of the Orphics was suggested by Nicolas Fréret in a memoir to
the Académie des Inscriptions (vol. 25) and taken up by C. F. Volney in
his very popular *Les Ruines, ou méditations sur les révolutions des empires*
(1791), where Fabre d'Olivet probably found it.

# VII. SURVEY OF CELESTIAL MUSIC

LET US PAUSE a moment on the celestial sphere, and, penetrating as far as prudence permits into the secrecy of the ancient sanctuaries, let us suppose that we are listening to one of the wise Eumolpids[93] speaking: "Seeing the seven primordial planets forming a sort of circle around a common hearth," he says, "the vulgar imagine that the earth is placed at the center of this hearth, and that it sees not only the planets turning around itself, but even the supreme sphere that encloses it; but this is mere appearance, a gross illusion of their senses that they take for a truth. It is prudent to leave them to their error until they can rid themselves of it; for as they cannot grasp the truth if it is presented to them before their mind is properly prepared, by relieving them of their error one would only be throwing them into chaos and making them incapable of guiding themselves through the darkness in

---

93. Fabre d'Olivet defines the Eumolpids as "perfect ones," the disciples of Orpheus, in *Histoire philosophique du genre humain* (1979), vol. I, p. 297 (English translation, p. 192), and gives his etymology of their name in *Les Vers dorés de Pythagore*, p. 73n. (not in the English translation) as coming from *eumolpos*, "*la voix accomplie*." Fabre d'Olivet called his own verse-form *vers eumolpiques*.

which they would suddenly be enveloped. The Earth
is no more at the center of the Universe than Jupiter
or Mercury; it is only a planet, like they. The Moon
has its place in the planetary order, and when the
initiates speak of the Moon, they always mean the
Earth, because they know that the Moon, the Earth,
and Tartarus, or the Earth of the Earth, are but one
and the same thing under three different names.[94] For
them it is the triple Hecate: Proserpine in the under-
world, Diana on the earth, and Phoebe in the heavens.
If the Earth is central, it is only when one considers it
as constituting a particular system within the universal system, and takes it as the tonic of a musical mode.
On the other hand, the philosophers, having seen that
the Earth cannot occupy the center of the Universe,
place the Sun there, and explain by mathematical abstractions the phenomena of the celestial motions.
But," the Eumolpid continues, "that is still only the
system of the Lesser Mysteries of which one now and
then permits a part to be divulged to the people, so as
to attack unconsciously the multitude of their errors.
Although it is certain that the Sun is infinitely better
placed at the center of the Universe than at any point
on the circumference, it is none the less true that this
star, seen from the Earth, should never be considered
as a planet. Listen carefully to the reason, and do not
reject without a lengthy examination what I am going
to tell you. It is that in its central place, it is invisible
to us. If it manifests itself to our eyes, it is by the
reflection of its light. The Sun that we see is only a
sensible image of the intelligible Sun,[95] which from

94. This statement is a summary of the cosmology of the Pythagorean
Philolaus.
95. A reference again to the doctrines of the emperor Julian concerning
the physical and the intelligible sun, here conflated with the Philolaic

the center imparts movement to the Universe and fills it with light. Those of its rays that reach us illuminate us only thanks to a sort of circumferential mirror that corporifies them and adapts them to the feebleness of our organs.

"It is not necessary to know any more of this for the understanding of the musical figure with which we are concerned, and it would be beside the point for me to go further into this matter. Suffice it for you to know that the calculations of our astronomers relating to movements, to mass, to the respective distances of the celestial bodies, to their inner nature, are excellent as far as physical relationships and civil usage are concerned, and deduced, for the most part, with rare talent; yet they are vain when one comes to apply them to knowledge of the truth. Calculations based on terrestrial illusions are never accurate except on that basis, and vanish as soon as one tries to detach them from it. The movements of the stars are a consequence of those attributed to the Earth, and have no other certitude. Thus if the Earth were not to have the motions the astronomers believe it to have, or if it has other motions, everything in their universal system would change instantly; they calculate distances by solar parallax, which is entirely unknown to them because they seek the center of that star where it is not, and they weigh masses by means of relations they establish between the Moon and the Earth, without knowing that since the Moon is in no way different from the Earth, these relations are identities; instead of two terms, as they believe, they never give them more than one.

scheme of the Sun as distinct from the Central Fire or Hearth of the Universe.

"For the rest, these calculations, although there is nothing true about them, are still very useful, as I have said, when one applies them solely to the necessities of life; they become vain or dangerous only when one tries to transfer them from the sensible to the intelligible, and to give them a universal existence which they lack. It would be the same if after having established, like our initiate sages, an intellectual system founded on celestial music, one tried to submit the results to the calculation of physical numbers. For knowing from the first principle that there is the ratio of a fourth between Saturn and the Sun, and between the Sun and the Moon—so that the Sun is the central and tonic point of the other two planets—does not enable one to express in physical numbers the respective distances of these luminaries, their size and movement, because the musical ratio of a fourth can be given by strings infinitely varying in length, thickness, and vibrations, according to their inner constitution and the more or less homogeneous nature of their parts.

"One must therefore avoid unwisely substituting one system for the other. The physical system serves to calculate by approximations that seem exact the apparent courses of the celestial bodies, and to predict the return of phenomena; the intellectual system, to make known by constant ratios the cause of these movements, and to evaluate the phenomenal illusions that they produce. The first is knowledge of the external and visible effects, the second of the internal and hidden principles. Science consists of uniting these systems and of using each for its own object. This is where true philosophy lies. In contemplating them both, this science teaches that the first of these systems, unvarying like the Cause of which it reveals the principle, disappears as the intellect is dimmed; while the other, bound to the variation of forms, changes with the times, peoples, and climates, so as to serve at least to enlighten people again in the moral darkness wherein their own will and the vicissitudes of Nature often plunge them."

After having meditated for a moment on this discourse of the Eumolpid, let us pass on to the diatonic development in music. This development works by opposing the fundamental strings that give the two primordial tones B and F.

| B | E | A | D | G | C | F |
|------|------|------|------|------|-----|-----|
| 4096 | 3072 | 2304 | 1728 | 1296 | 972 | 729 |

| F | C | G | D | A | E | B |
|------|------|------|------|------|-----|-----|
| 5832 | 3888 | 2592 | 1728 | 1152 | 728 | 512 |

We find in the opposition of these two strings the ratios existing between all the diatonic intervals, and the identity of the tones is irresistibly proven by the union established on the D, which is the median tone of the two strings. In the planetary spheres, this unison on D corresponds to the planet Mars.

If we now transpose the strings B and F to their higher octaves, always moving them by the appropriate contrary progressions, we will forthwith obtain the series of diatonic tones following the rank given them by Nature.

### SATURNIAN DIATONIC SYSTEM

| Saturn | Jupiter | Mars | Sun | Venus | Mercury | Moon |
|--------|---------|------|-----|-------|---------|------|
| B | C | D | E | F | G | A |

FABRE D'OLIVET

## CYPRIAN DIATONIC SYSTEM

| Venus | Mercury | Moon | Saturn | Jupiter | Mars | Sun |
|-------|---------|------|--------|---------|------|-----|
| F | G | A | B | C | D | E |

From all that I have said it follows that the diatonic tones as we have received them from the Latins and Greeks are in no way arbitrary, either in their ratios or in their rank, and that the Egyptians, who equated the number to that of the planets and who ranked them in the same order, followed in this regard a respectable tradition founded on truth, or else were themselves inspired by a profound wisdom. These tones, as we are convinced, owe their identity to the contrary unfoldings of two principles, and their ranking order to the reconciliation of these same principles. Their ratios are established by mathematical proportions of rigorous exactitude, of which one can alter nothing without throwing everything into confusion. We can thus accept them in all certitude and make them the unshakeable basis of our system.[96]

## SATURNIAN DIATONIC SYSTEM — Fundamental string B

| B | C | D | E | F | G | A |
|---|---|---|---|---|---|---|
| from 2048 | to 1944 | to 1728 | to 1536 | to 1458 | to 1296 | to 1152 |

96. These figures give the two intervals of Pythagorean diatonic tuning: all whole tones are in the ratio 9:8, all semitones (*leimmas*, or "leftovers"), in the ratio 256:243.

## CYPRIAN DIATONIC SYSTEM — Fundamental string F

| F | G | A | B | C | D | E |
|---|---|---|---|---|---|---|
| from 2926 | to 2592 | to 2304 | to 2048 | to 1944 | to 1728 | to 1536 |

The only thing still left to mention about this diatonic order concerns celestial music. One should recall that the Egyptians, having represented the planetary septenary by the fundamental string B and conceived its ascending development according to the progression by fourths, considered this progression as divine and spiritual, and gave to the progression by fifths the name of terrestrial and corporeal; they also preferred the diatonic order given by this string, all the more since it assigns to the planets the same order as they have in ethereal space,[97] as follows:

| Saturn | Jupiter | Mars | Sun | Venus | Mercury | Moon |
|--------|---------|------|-----|-------|---------|------|
| B | C | D | E | F | G | A |

It is because of the idea that the Egyptians had of the superiority of the Saturnian principle B over the Cyprian F, that they made its progression by fourths govern the seven days of the week, and its diatonic course the 24 hours of the day, as Dion Cassius says expressly in his *Roman History*.[98]

97. That is, the order working outward from the Earth considered as center: presumably different from the order of the physical solar system, which is heliocentric.

98. *Roman History*, XXXVII, 18.

Here is this order for the days of the week:

| Saturday | Sunday | Monday | Tuesday | Wednesday | Thursday | Friday |
|----------|--------|--------|---------|-----------|----------|--------|
| Saturn | Sun | Moon | Mars | Mercury | Jupiter | Venus |
| B | E | A | D | G | C | F |

For the hours of morning and afternoon:

| | 1 | 2 | 3 | 4 | 5 | 6 | 7 | 8 | 9 | 10 | 11 | 12 | |
|---|---|---|---|---|---|---|---|---|---|---|---|---|---|
| Saturday Day of Saturn | B | C | D | E | F | G | A | B | C | D | E | F | a.m. |
| | G | A | B | C | D | E | F | G | A | B | C | D | p.m. |
| Sunday Day of the Sun | E | F | G | A | B | C | D | E | F | G | A | B | a.m. |
| | C | D | E | F | G | A | B | C | D | E | F | G | p.m. |
| Monday Day of the Moon | A | B | C | D | E | F | G | A | B | C | D | E | a.m. |
| | F | G | A | B | C | D | E | F | G | A | B | C | p.m. |
| Tuesday Day of Mars | D | E | F | G | A | B | C | D | E | F | G | A | a.m. |
| | B | C | D | E | F | G | A | B | C | E | F | G | p.m. |
| Wedn'day Day of Mercury | G | A | B | C | D | E | F | G | A | B | C | D | a.m. |
| | E | F | G | A | B | C | D | E | F | G | A | B | p.m. |
| Thursday Day of Jupiter | C | D | E | F | G | A | B | C | D | E | F | G | a.m. |
| | A | B | C | D | E | F | G | A | B | C | D | E | p.m. |
| Friday Day of Venus | F | G | A | B | C | D | E | F | G | A | B | C | a.m. |
| | D | E | F | G | A | B | C | D | E | F | G | A | p.m. |

Thus, by making the musical diatonic septenary operate within the harmonic septenary, applied to the seven days of the week after dividing each of these days into twice twelve hours, the Egyptians found a way to distinguish the different and respective relationships of the two principles B and F, which had combined their actions in the zodiacal number 12, and demonstrated the identity of their products by forming a series of similar diatonic tones; then they distinguished these tones within the horary number 24 by coordinating them in different ways among themselves, and opposing them to each other according to whether they were taken alternatively as the principle of a series, or, musically speaking, as the tonic of a mode. The result of this new movement is that one can recognize seven diatonic modes, which form fourteen since one can consider them as primordial or secondary; but, as I shall explain later, these seven primordial modes are reduced to five, because the principles B and F, acting separately, can never constitute true modes in the meaning I give to this term.

**F. D.**
*France Musicale,* **16 June 1850**

# VIII. THE MUSICAL SYSTEM OF THE CHINESE

AFTER THE INDIAN EMPIRE had been broken up,[99] there appeared in its midst an extraordinary man who undertook to rehabilitate it by purifying its religion and resolving the difficulties that had arisen concerning the first cause of the Universe; this man, called Rama, succeeded in his plans, and although his edifice crumbled in its turn in the hands of his feeble successors, he nonetheless earned immortal glory by raising it. This Rama, surnamed "Deo-Naoush"[100] from "Deva-Naoush," the same as "Issaoura" whose altars he everywhere raised up under this name, is the same as he whom the Greeks call Dionysos. Now according to the calculations of Arrian and Pliny, more than 6,400 years elapsed between the epoch of Dionysos and the time when Alexander of Macedonia attempted the conquest of India. The expedition of Alexander took place, as we know, 326 years before our era; so

99. The version of prehistory assumed in this chapter — and throughout the book — is Fabre d'Olivet's own, expounded in his *De l'état social de l'homme*, 2 vols. (Paris, 1822), republished 1824 with the new title *Histoire philosophique du genre humain*.

100. Several chapters of the *Histoire philosophique du genre humain* are devoted to the Druid and Indian hero Rama. See vol. I, pp. 199ff. (English translation, pp. 106ff.).

that by adding the 1,825 years[101] from then until the present, we will find that we cannot admit less than 8,551 years between ourselves and Rama. This divine man, according to the Brahmins, was one of the incarnations of Vishnu and appeared at the end of the Second Age, thirty or thirty-five generations after Bharata; which at thirty to thirty-three years per generation makes about ten centuries. All of this gives nearly 9,000 years of antiquity to the system of Bharata, which may lead one to regard the troubles to which it gave birth and which caused the breakup of the last Universal Empire as having erupted for the first time 5,600 years ago.

Although the Chinese are, of all peoples, the ones who began earliest on to write their civil history, their annals are far from reaching to the epoch of which I have been speaking. The authentic dates that they give do not go back beyond the Hsia Dynasty, twenty-three or twenty-four centuries before Christ, that is, about 4,200 years before the present.

The 4,300 or 4,400 years that must, by my calculations, separate this dynasty from the expedition of Rama that momentarily united the *Tchandra douep*[102] or China to the Indian Empire are filled with allegorical accounts referring not to human personages but to moral and cosmogonic beings, as was the custom of the time. One reads there, for example, that at first the color white reigned alone in the Universe to the

101. This date and those that follow are altered in the review to the year 1843; the year 1825, that of the death of Fabre d'Olivet, is reinstated here in conformity with the edition of Philipon; in 1822 the work on *Music* was announced by the author as due to appear imminently (see *Etat social de l'homme*, vol. I, notes to pp. 189, 264, and 268). [JP] See note 13 to the Translator's Introduction.

102. Defined as "the country of the masculine moon" in *op. cit.*, vol. I, p. 263 (English translation, p. 163).

exclusion of all others, and that it was only in the time
of Kuang Chheng-tzu[103] that the color yellow appeared
and took ascendancy over its rival. Now the color
white here signifies either the Indian Empire, which
carried it as its standard, or else Rama himself, whose
name in Sanskrit signifies brilliant whiteness, whereas
the color yellow characterizes the Chinese Empire,
which always had that as its distinctive color. The
very name of Kuang Chheng-tzu signifies that it is to
him that attaches the moral principle of the empire
whose symbol is the color yellow. One finds, in the
same allegorical style, that it was Chu Jung[104] who
invented the music whose powerful melody served to
unite the Chinese people, improve their mores, and
make them cherish his laws. The name of this moral
personage indicates only the external principle on
which this music was founded, a principle that we
will examine without delay.

The Chinese historians unanimously agree that the
fundamental principle on which their empire was built
— now the greatest and the most populous on earth
— was that of music. Pan Ku, one of the most celebrated of them, formally declares that the doctrine of
the *Chings*, the sacred books of the nation, rests entirely on this science, represented in these books as
the expression and the image of the union of Earth
with Heaven. After Chu Jung, Fu-Hsi, and Huang-Ti,
who are evidently moral and allegorical beings, those
whom the Chinese regard as the authors of their mus-

---

103. An associate of the "Yellow Emperor" Huang-Ti; a recluse. In
*Histoire philosophique du genre humain*, vol. I, p. 263 (English translation,
p. 163) it is "Fo-hi" (Fu-Hsi) who is said to have taken the color yellow as
his ensign.

104. Fabre d'Olivet gives "Tchou-Joung-Che," presumably the legendary
Chu Jung, variously called the God of Fire and a minister under Huang-Ti.

ical system are Ling Lun, Khuei, and Pin-Mou-Kia. The epoch of Ling Lun, the most celebrated of the three, cannot be exactly fixed. Presumably it is not far distant from that of the very foundation of the Empire, which goes back as I have said 8,000 to 8,500 years. The *Yo Ching*, the sacred book that contained the laws of music, has not survived the violent religious or political upheavals that China has suffered at various times. It is believed that every copy was given to the flames by order of Chhin Shih Huang Ti when this monarch, angered by the obstinacy with which the scholars persisted in rejecting his new institutions, ordered the burning of all the ancient books from which they claimed their right to oppose him. (This event took place 237 years before the Christian era.)

The fragments that survived in memory were carefully collected after the extinction of the Chhin Dynasty by the succeeding Han Dynasty, which gloried in reestablishing what its predecessors had attempted to destroy and made great efforts to enable the ancient music to flourish again; but the troubles and civil war that ensued did not permit it to complete its work and threw everything into fresh disorder. It was not until long afterward that a prince of the Ming Dynasty (the Ming Dynasty began in the year 1370 of the Common Era), named Tsai-yü,[105] an enthusiast for this science, undertook to restore it to its ancient glory by rehabilitating it in its original state; he surrounded himself for this purpose with all the musical experts, theoretical and practical, that China could offer, and investigated all the national monuments to which his rank facilitated entry. The result of his labors was the mus-

___

105. Prince Tsai-yü Chu, 1536–1611, author of *Lü-lü ching-i* (Essentials of Music), which formulates equal temperament.

ical system that is still followed today in this vast empire and which, by unanimous consent of scholars, does not differ from that of Ling Lun, and above all rests on the same principles, considered as sacred from the most remote antiquity, as is indisputably proven by the sacred hymns sung from time immemorial by the Emperor himself at the Feast of the Ancestors.

This principle, called *Kung*, that is, luminous hearth, center where all ends and whence all emanates, corresponds to the tone we call F. It is assimilated in the universal order to the *Tien*, that is, the masculine nature, and depends on the *Yang* or perfect odd number represented mysteriously by the unbroken line, as opposed to the *Yin*, which is represented by the divided line.[106]

The pipe that gives this fundamental tone, called above all others the *huang chung*, supreme dominant tone, resplendent, yellow in color, bears itself the generic name *yo*, which means "music," of which it is the regulator.[107] From its origin, and still today, its diameter is that of three grains of large millet, its circumference nine, and its entire capacity two hundred. Each grain of this millet, called in Chinese *shu*, is equivalent to what they call a *fên*, or a line.[108] As this pipe which sounds the *huang chung* has always served in China as the basis of all measures both of surfaces and of volumes, one can see with what attention the government must have watched over its con-

106. Fabre d'Olivet had explained this in *Les Vers dorés de Pythagore*, p. 199n. (English translation, p. 19n.), mentioning in the same note that he would explain the subject further when he came to speak of music.

107. It is remarkable that the word *yo*, which means "music" in Chinese, also signifies the *sacred mountain* to which this people attaches its origin, and serves to express *its will*. [FdO]

108. A *ligne*, or line: obsolete measure of 1/12 inch; in China the *fên* is 1/10 of the *tshun*, or foot.

servation. But fearing lest revolutions might have brought some changes to its form and size, Prince Tsai-yü neglected nothing that might ensure its primordial integrity. Having found through his researches that the measure used by the Hsia Dynasty must have been the same as that used by the Founders of the Empire, he took as a model the musical foot whose description he had read in ancient fragments of books and whose imprint he had seen on certain ruins of old monuments, and caused an exact model of it to be forged in brass. This replica, after receiving imperial approval, became a universal metrical type for all China. Even today it is to this tone that all instruments and voices are tuned; by its capacity all liquid measures are determined; by its length everything is measured that has to do with the geometric division of surfaces, the dimensions of solids, lengths, and weight. Legal copies of this important prototype, carefully preserved in all the towns, engraved on all the public monuments, are everywhere visible to the people. Those which represent the imperial model are square in form, having four equal sides. The interior, which is hollow and perfectly round, is as I have said nine lines in circumference. One of its sides is divided into nine inches of nine lines each, making eighty-one lines in all: it is the *musical* foot. The other side is divided into ten inches of ten lines each, making in all one hundred lines: it is the *calculating* foot. The first is called *Lü-chhih* and the second *Tou-chhih*. The *Lü-chhih*, according to the Chinese experts who have worked on this subject, is the foot that Huang-Ti used; it should only be employed for the calculation of intellectual things. The *Tou-chhih* is the foot used by the great Yü and the Hsia Dynasty; it should be applied to the calculation of physical things.

Thus it is from the fundamental *Kung* or from the principle F that everything in China, both in the moral and the physical sphere, receives its number, its measure, and its weight. It is to this unique principle that everything is related; and — a wonderful thought — it is by examining this principle whose form in the pipe that produces it has not varied for eight thousand years that one can know the idea of the founders of this empire, perceive its connection with the laws that regulate the Universe, and even appreciate the exact pitch they gave to their songs on the musical scale. What is perhaps no less marvelous, and which nonetheless results from such an institution, is that thanks to this very principle F, recognized as sacred and irresistibly fixed in form, a people of no less than twenty million souls has the same weights, the same measures, and uses the same vocal intonations in the same passages of their songs.[109] The resemblance of what happens in China today to what happened in Egypt in the time of Plato is too extraordinary to be the effect of chance, and I do not doubt that a judicious reader who grasps the connection will see the convincing proof of all that I have said.

### *France Musicale*, 24 September 1843

Note [JP]: This article is reproduced in part and almost literally in the Dictionary of Escudier, article "Chinois (Système Musical des)," completed by the addition of the following:

Now that we know the principle on which the

---

109. Chinese uniformity (in literary standards) is also praised in Fabre d'Olivet's *Discours*, p. 13.

Chinese musical system of Ling Lun is founded, and the manner in which it is established, let us see under what ratios this famous man conceived its development, and how he made the diatonic and chromatic tones ensue which he put into his system.

Ling Lun, taking the fundamental string F as the generating tone of all the other tones and sounding it loudly either on the musical stone *chhing* or on the harmonious bronze *chung*,[110] heard in the reverberation of these bodies several tones analogous to the generating tone, among which he recognized that the first and most lasting were the octave above the fundamental and its double fifth or its twelfth;[111] thus he was led to believe that the development of sonorous bodies in general occurred with a combined series that made them follow simultaneously a double and a triple progression, double as from 1 to 2 or from 4 to 8 to produce its octave, and triple as from 1 to 3 and from 4 to 12 to produce its twelfth. This combined series, which comprised the opposing faculties of even and odd, convinced him all the more since it failed to admit any new principle, and allowed him apparently to make everything flow from unity. We say apparently, because in supposing this heterogeneous and simultaneous series of 1 to 2 and 1 to 3, the system where it reigns to the exclusion of that of 3 to 4 will always lack the descending chromatic and enharmonic genera. Rameau, who more than eight thousand years after Ling Lun wished to make it the basis of his musical system, starting from the same experience,

---

110. Fabre d'Olivet gives these instruments as *yuhing* and *lien-tchoung*; current orthography (as in the *New Grove Dictionary of Music and Musicians*) reads *ging* and *zhong*. Wherever possible, the translator has followed the spellings of Joseph Needham (*Science and Civilization in China*).
111. That is, he heard the first and second partial tones (harmonics).

was forced to have recourse to a false temperament which mutilates all the tones, and which, twenty times proposed in China, was twenty times rejected; because the savants of that nation, although they had long been aware of the void in their system, preferred to keep it pure though incomplete rather than spoil one of its parts in order to supply the missing one.

In the epoch when Ling Lun proposed his unique principle, driven by the schismatic spirit that dominated him, he could not find a better theory, and had to agree that despite its insufficiencies it still presents great beauties and above all shows a great perspicacity of mind in its inventor.

One of the writers whose works are able to give the best indications on the music of the Chinese is Père Amyot.[112]

112. J. J. M. Amiot (or Amyot), missionary to Peking, author of *Mémoires concernant l'histoire, les sciences et les arts des Chinois* (Paris, 1776–91). Fabre d'Olivet drew heavily on his sixth volume, on Chinese music, part of which had been in circulation in manuscript since 1754, hence available also to Abbé Roussier.

# IX. THE MUSICAL SYSTEM OF THE GREEKS[113]

WHEN THE MUSIC of the Greeks comes into question, we do not suffer for want of writers: on the contrary, it is the writers who are the problem, because even after reading them all it is difficult to know what they were trying to say, thanks to the incoherence that permeates their works and the contradictions into which they fall at every step, not only with each other but even with themselves. Their obscurity and want of agreement come in general from the fact that they knew neither the origin nor the principles of the science.

Since this origin and these principles are known to us today, we have only to work out their consequences in order to know the exact nature of the music of the Greeks, and to be able to explain effortlessly all the

---

113. The first part of this chapter is reproduced in part, and almost literally, in the Dictionary of Escudier under "Grecs anciens (Musique des)."

The second part, completed by two notes [our notes 122, 123], was reproduced in *La France Musicale* on 25 March 1849 under the title "Orphée" and the signature F. D., from "Orpheus is the first man among the Greeks who created an epoch . . ." to "When Pythagoras appeared in Greece. . . ." [JP]

facts that the history of these celebrated peoples has transmitted to us on this subject.

First let us recall an important point. Europe, partly savage, was like all the rest of the hemisphere a dependency of the Indian Empire until the schism of the Shepherd Kings;[114] thereupon it was separated at a stroke and passed under the dominion of the Phoenicians together with the countries of Asia and Africa bordering the Mediterranean. This race of brilliant navigators and bold merchants wandered along the coasts, seizing existing colonies, establishing new ones, and penetrating as far as they could inland. The names which they gave to their new foundations were all drawn from their own mythology or the symbols of their religion. Their most successful and extensive colonies included at one and the same time the Thracians, the Dacians, the Tuscans, and the Etruscans: names which differ only in dialect, and which all reduce to the same: the primitive name of Thrace, which in Phoenician signifies *ethereal space*.[115]

Greece was not at first distinguished from Thrace: its name is the same, only more restrained and less emphatic because of the different initial letter. The name of Ionia which was given it later, designating the particular symbol of the Ionic sect, it had in common with all the Phoenician possessions both in Europe and Asia.

Greece, or if you will Thrace — for at that time one

114. See *Histoire philosophique du genre humain*, vol. I, pp. 252ff. (English translation, pp. 154ff.). The "Shepherd Kings" are here identified with the schismatic sect of Irshou, devotees of the feminine principle above the masculine one, whose symbol was the *yoni* (female generative organ), hence the name "Ionia" (see below). See also the extract from this book given as Appendix F.

115. This etymology is also given in *Les Vers dorés de Pythagore expliqués*, 1813 ed., p. 16. (Not in the English translation.)

was no different from the other — thus received its music from the hands of the Phoenicians, who communicated their system little by little as the circumstances and the state of civilization allowed. In order to understand this system properly and follow its developments, it is necessary to know that the word "lyre," since applied to one particular musical instrument, was at first purely a generic term given to music itself, and transferred by extension to the scientific instrument by means of which the laws of music were determined. (This Greek word *lyra* derived from the same root as the Phoenician word *sirah*, which expresses everything that is harmonious and concordant.) What was understood by the three-stringed lyre was not the musical instrument which one played, but that which constituted the fundamental tuning. It was from the moment when the theoretical instrument was confused with the practical one that understanding was lost.

The three-stringed lyre of which Diodorus Siculus writes designated the most ancient system, that of the conjunct tetrachords. [BCDE overlapping with EFGA] These three strings were B, E, A. The four-stringed lyre treated by Boethius indicated the system of disjunct tetrachords [EFGA, BCDE]. These four strings were E, A, B, E, or else A, D, E, A. To talk of the "lyre" was to indicate the system, which was to indicate everything: for since the disposition of a tetrachord was mathematically fixed in the diatonic genus, one could not go wrong.

This arrangement within every tetrachord, going from high to low in the Phoenician manner, was of two successive whole tones and a semitone. The Greeks, as long as they were no different from the Thracians, had no other melody; everything was in-

cluded for them in the musical interval of the tetrachords, set out as I have said.

In the two systems of conjunct and disjunct tetrachords, the mode fluctuated between the tonics A and
E, resting for preference on A, which very much con-
forms to the ideas of this mode consecrated to the
feminine nature. However, since the final at the bot-
tom of the system of conjunct tetrachords ended on B,
allowing momentary dominance to the principle assimilated to the masculine nature, the Phoenicians
wished to eliminate this dominance and for this purpose added at the lower end a string tuned a double
octave below the highest note of the disjunct tetrachord system, that is, a fundamental A.

In this way they taught the Greeks their favorite
mode, the Locrian, the "song of alliance," known particularly under the epithet of *linos*, the lunar, and
celebrated for its melancholy effect. By means of the
addition of these two strings, the two systems were
forged into a single one, differing in only one point
from that of the Hindus, as I have already explained:
a point that seems at first unimportant, though it involves very serious consequences with regard to the
principle from which it emanates. This point is that
the string B flat, found in the tetrachord *synnemenon*,
forms part of the system in that it is a diatonic tone;
and henceforth effacing the B natural as its principle,
it makes it subordinate to the F, which now becomes
the dominant one. These ideas, as we know, were
those of the Phoenicians and of all the nations called
Ionians or Amazonians.

This musical system which we may call Ionian, having reached perfection, remained thus for a long time
among the Thracians. It seems that all the modulation
these peoples had was restricted to passing from the

conjunct to the disjunct tetrachord, or vice versa. Often they did not modulate at all; then they sang on the lyre of three or four strings according to whether they wished to use the diapason of the seventh or the octave. As the melody was contained in the range of the tetrachord, the songs were facile and uncomplicated. It often sufficed the singer to sound the principal strings of the lyres, B, E, A or E, A, B, E, in order to improvise their filling-out with secondary tones.[116] What confirms this opinion is the way in which certain ancient Greek poems are notated. Among those of the Vatican Library[117] some have been found in which the end of each verse is marked by a vocal and an instrumental letter, placed immediately after one another; evidently the intention of the poet or musician is that one should begin to sing the verse on the designated string, or to stop there, leaving the singer free to fill out the rest at will. Thus the theoretical lyre may very well have been vocal, existing with three or four strings always plucked open; but from the moment it became practical and instrumental it was necessary to augment the number of strings, which gave birth to the harp, the epigonion, the psalterion, etc., or alternatively adding a fingerboard where the fingers could stop each string and make it sound the different notes of the tetrachord which it represented, leading to the invention of the cithara, the barbiton, the mandora, etc.

It would be hard to say how long Ionian music remained in this simple state. All one can reasonably

116. Fabre d'Olivet had suggested this in his third letter on Greek music, *Correspondance des amateurs et professeurs de musique*, 25 August 1804 (see Translator's Introduction).

117. Fabre d'Olivet cited these manuscripts in his third letter on Greek music (see previous note), but I have not been able to identify them.

affirm in this regard is that its variations followed those of the sect which had adopted it as a symbol of its alliance. I have said that this sect rapidly began to divide. Almost every one of the peoples that caused this division laid claim to a music different from all the others, for since music had been one of the first causes of the original schism, it must have figured strongly in the formation of the particular sects that were spawned thereby. Thus were formed a host of different systems, among which the principal ones were called "Lydian," "Phrygian," and "Dorian," after the peoples who adopted them. These systems were not precisely the same as the Hindus understood under the name of *ragas*, nor what we understand today by modes, because in place of a series of seven notes contained within one octave, they contained up to sixteen within the interval of the double octave. These systems, as I have shown, consisted of a series of conjunct and disjunct tetrachords, and varied in the sequence of those tetrachords, some by the placing of the semitone, others by simple transposition up or down. Such is the confusion caused by the large number of these systems, and so careless the way in which they are distinguished by the writers who have treated them, that it is impossible today to ascertain even of the three principal ones whether the tonic of the Lydian was E or C, that of the Dorian C or E.

On this point there is not a single author who fails to contradict another one, and frequently himself as well. But in this melee of contrary opinions I have found two authorities who have determined me in ascribing to the Lydian mode the tonic E, and to the Dorian the tonic C. The first is Aristoxenus,[118] who

118. An interpretation of *Harmonics*, II, 37.

says that the Dorians performed the same song a tone lower than the Phrygians, and the latter a tone lower than the Lydians. The second authority, confirming this, is the judicious Saumasius, who tells us in his *Commentary on the Comedies of Terence* that the music used for these comedies was played on flutes appropriate to each mode; some using the Phrygian mode, others the Dorian, lower than the Phrygian; and the third kind the Lydian, higher than the other two modes. Zarlino in Italy and Fux in Germany followed this opinion, as did J.-J. Rousseau in France, who cites Ptolemy on this subject. Otherwise the etymology of the names, together with the many consequences that follow from all this, must confirm this opinion.

## *France Musicale*, 1 October 1843

**IXa. Orpheus[119] and Pythagoras**   After all that I have said so far, I think I have no need to explain why Amphion, Marsyas, and Thamyris, who are said to be the inventors of the three systems Lydian, Phrygian, and Dorian, were by no means the physical personages they are taken to be: one must realize that at this remote epoch history did not concern itself with individuals. These three names signify moral, not human beings: they designate as inventors of these systems the actual ideas that presided over their invention.

Thus Amphion, who presides over the Lydian system (meaning the one of the female generative faculty), means precisely the national or metropolitan voice of Ionia; Marsyas, inventor of the Phrygian (the

119. There is much on Orpheus as codifier of rhythm in Fabre d'Olivet's *Dissertation*, pp. 16f.

system of the leaders of flocks or of the Shepherd Kings), represents the fiery spirit, the ardor of the warrior; and Thamyris, who rules the Dorian (that of liberty or strength) designates the light of the twin stars.

It was a great musical revolution when first one dared to separate the tetrachords that, according to ancient and sacred laws, must remain forever conjoined. This revolution, whose consequences were weightier than one could ever imagine, had its source in the doctrine of Krishna concerning universal hermaphrodism.[120] This doctrine had already had the most striking success; it was accepted in Libya, in Egypt, in Arabia, and in part of Phoenicia, and thence easily penetrated Europe, where it had already made considerable progress among the Thracians. The Ionians, justifiably alarmed by a doctrine that threatened to restrict their influence and fearing to see the utter collapse of their empire, already weakened as it was rent apart, attempted to resist its passage; but it was too late. The high priesthood pronounced its anathema in vain: all of Greece arose and thenceforth dissociated itself from Thrace properly so-called, which remained faithful to the metropolis. Altar was raised against altar, and Mount Parnassus chosen to replace the holy mountain of Thrace, seat of the sovereign Pontiff who was no longer recognized.[121] There they built the town of Delphi, designated as the holy city under the name *Pytho*. It was there that the new sect, claiming to be guided by *Olen*, the universal spirit, placed the famous Omphalos, symbol of the divine hermaphrodism, and took as its object of worship the Sun and Moon united

120. See *Histoire philosophique du genre humain*, vol. I, pp. 277ff. (English translation, pp. 175ff.).
121. In Fabre d'Olivet's *Dissertation*, p. 19, Orpheus himself is named the Pontiff of Delphi.

in a single being, known at first by the name *Oetolinos*. This revolution, by forever separating Greece from Phoenicia and isolating the latter from Thrace, has exercised a vast influence on the destinies of Europe; it deserves some day to occupy the pens of historians.

Incomplete as they were, the Greek chromatic and enharmonic genera had in their novelty a powerful effect as employed in the hands of Orpheus. At this name, to which so many brilliant memories are associated, I feel stirring within me the desire to reenter the fields of history in order to raise there a monument to the glory of the divine man who bore it. But this would be to trespass too far beyond the limits I have set myself, this desire to do for modern times what I have done for Antiquity. Suffice it here to draw the line of demarcation that separates allegorical and moral history from the positive and civic type. Orpheus is the first man among the Greeks who created an epoch, by placing himself in the center of a moral sphere whose influence is still felt among us after more than thirty-three centuries.[122] Instructed by the Egyptians, initiated into their most secret mysteries, he rose in Greece to the rank of prophet and supreme pontiff. He was capable of uniting in a single cult twenty hostile nations, divided in their religious opinions as well as in their secular laws, and founded that admirable Amphictyonic League[123] whose decrees were sanctioned by the sovereign Pontiff of Delphi. It was he who created the magnificent Greek mythology

122. Orpheus was a Thracian; his name, too, is still Phoenician. It comes from Aor-ropheh, "luminous Medicine"; that is to say, the light of Medicine or Salvation, both moral and physical. [FdO]
123. That is to say, the union of the metropolitan voices of the native earth. [FdO]

which, despite the persistent efforts of an intolerant and fanatical religion, still shines through the ridiculous rags in which it has been wrapped to animate all our arts and rule our poetry.

The signal service rendered by Orpheus to Greek music was to base all the systems on a single one, and to distinguish, under the name of modes, what before him had been called systems. It is generally believed that he admitted only three modes in a single system.[124] These primitive modes were the Lydian, the Phrygian, and the Dorian, whose tonics were, in descending order, E, D, C. Some wished by dividing each of the two whole tones E, D and D, C into two intervals, using E flat and C sharp, to give rise to two additional modes, the Ionian and Aeolian, which would then only have been simple transpositions. Others, among them the elder Bacchius and Ptolemy, assure us that the modes admitted by Orpheus were seven in number; but they agree neither on the order nor on the names of these modes. Finally, some others established fifteen modes: five primitive (Lydian, Aeolian, Ionian, Phrygian or Iastian,[125] and Dorian); five upper secondaries, called by the term *hyper*, and five lower secondaries, called by the term *hypo*. But it is evident that these fifteen modes did not exist at all in Orpheus' time, in which also I am persuaded that the transposition of the modes from semitone to semitone was unknown.

It was only after Pythagoras that this transposition could have taken place, when that great man, having

---

124. In the article published in 1849 is added: "and three genera in each mode." [JP]

125. In the article published in 1849: "Iustien" in place of "iastien." [JP]

THE SECRET LORE OF MUSIC

penetrated to the depth of the Egyptian sanctuaries
with a courage and a constancy[126] unequaled before
then, learned and taught to his disciples the principles
of this science[127] and showed them how to fill out the
musical system with an uninterrupted series of diatonic, chromatic, and enharmonic intervals following
rigorous mathematical progressions.

When Pythagoras[128] appeared in Greece about nine
centuries after Orpheus, rich in all the learning of
Africa and Asia, he found the memory of philosophy
practically extinct in men's minds, and his most beautiful teachings were either misunderstood or attributed to fantastic origins. The petty arrogance of be-
lieving themselves autochthonous, owing nothing to
neighboring nations, had perverted all the Greeks'
ideas. In Crete they placed the tomb of Zeus, the living
god; they insisted that the divine spirit Dionysos had
been born in a village of Boeotia, and the universal
father Apollo on a small island in the Archipelago. A
thousand absurdities of this kind were spewed forth,
and when the masses who believed them became sovereign, the wisest were arrogantly condemned to believe them, too. The Mysteries, established in order to
make known the truth, were now opened to an exces-
sive number of initiates and lost their influence; the
hierophants, intimidated or corrupted, held their peace

126. Variant of the article published in 1849: "with heroic courage and
indefatigable constancy." [JP]
127. In the article published in 1849 is added: "residing in the universal
quaternary." [JP]
128. This paragraph and the next are almost identical with a passage in
Histoire philosophique du genre humain, vol. I, pp. 311ff. (English translation, pp. 205f.), while the mention of autochthonous pretensions is also
found in Dissertation, p. 23.

and thus consecrated the lie. Truth had of necessity either to die altogether or another means had to be found for its preservation.

Pythagoras was the man to whom this secret was revealed. He did for science what Lycurgus had done for liberty. That legislator had instituted in a single area of Greece a convent of soldiers against whom the Persian despotism would be shattered. This philosopher founded a secret assembly of wise and religious men who, dispersing themselves through Europe, Asia, and even Africa, combatted there the ignorance and impiety that threatened to become universal. The services he rendered to humanity were immense.

The sect he created, not altogether extinct even today, cutting like a beam of light through the accumulated darkness inflicted on us by the barbarian invasions, the fall of the Roman Empire, and the necessary erection of an intolerant and superstitious religion, has facilitated a thousandfold the restoration of the sciences and spared us several centuries of labor.

It is this that has advanced all the physical sciences, revived chemistry, freed astronomy from the absurd prejudices that arrested its progress, taught us the importance of geometry and mathematics, and given guidelines to natural history. It has equally influenced the progress of the moral sciences, but with less success on account of the obstacles it has encountered in the gloomy metaphysics of the schools. It is to the writings of this learned sect and to certain fortunate circumstances that I owe my rediscovery of the true principles of music and the fact that I have succeeded with their help in writing about this science as I have done, following with a rectitude that doubtless will not have escaped the sagacious reader its systematic history among most nations of the earth for the period of twelve hundred thousand years.[129]

*France Musicale,* **8 October 1843**

---

129. The *Histoire philosophique du genre humain* claims to cover only the past twelve thousand years, not twelve hundred thousand. Perhaps "douze cent mille ans" is a misprint.

# X. The Musical System
## of the Eastern Christians

WE CAN PRESUME that in ancient times the musical
system of the Orientals possessed some method of
notation, for of the Egyptians, the Phoenicians, and
the Greeks (whose music much influenced that of the
Persians), the Egyptians, as we know, used the seven
vowels, and the others all the letters of the alphabet.
But after a series of revolutions that several times
overwhelmed Asia and Africa, it seems that the memory of this method was altogether lost in the East; at
least, it is certain that neither the Arabs nor the Persians knew of any signs for notating their music before
a certain Demetrius Cautemir, who tried in 1673 to
have the numerals used for this purpose. His invention, which had some success in Turkey and particularly in Constantinople, is still by no means generally
adopted in Persia or Arabia. Egypt itself seems to have
remained altogether ignorant of it, from what one
hears from the French who have visited that country.[130] These writers say that the first time the Egyp-

---

130. He refers here to the savants who accompanied Napoleon's Egyptian campaign in 1798–99, notably Guillaume André Villoteau, from whose

tians saw the French musicians writing down a tune while they sang it, and then playing it after them, they thought that there was magic in this simple procedure. That proves how neglected musical science is in Egypt, and confirms the assertion of these same writers when they describe Egyptian musical practice as a blind routine that is becoming more and more degenerate.

The musical systems of the Eastern Christians, varying according to their sects, are quite distant from that of the Arabs, the Persians, and the Turks, nor does their notation resemble that of which I have been speaking.

The ETHIOPIANS, who deserve first rank among these Eastern Christians, use alphabetical characters to notate their music; but these characters, which sometimes form a word of one or two syllables, indicate the intervals between the tones rather than the pitches themselves. Thus *he* means the rising semitone, or the sharp; *se* the lowered semitone, or the flat; *ka* the whole tone; *ha* the minor third; *wa* the major third; *e* the fourth; *zahe* the fifth, etc., etc. The musical system of these Christians, which they are certain was inspired by the Holy Spirit through a holy person named Jared, has three modes: the mode *guez*, corresponding to the lunar mode, a plagal modulation having its final on E; the mode *ezel*, corresponding to the solar, a plagal modulation having its final on E or F; lastly the mode *avaraï*, the most solemn of all since it is intended for the great feasts, which is a mixture of the solar and the mercurial, having its final on E or G. The chant of the Ethiopians, formerly very simple,

*Recherches sur l'analogie de la musique* (see note 53) nearly all of this chapter is derived.

is nowadays loaded with ornaments like that of the Arabs. One can judge this peculiar change it has undergone by comparing a verse given about 150 years ago by Kircher[131] and since republished with the ornaments that have been added to it. One can see in place of a solemn and majestic chant a twisted, mannered chant without any expressivity. All the sacred chants of the Ethiopians and Abyssinians are of this type.

The COPTS, who are the descendants of the ancient Egyptians, have a music even worse than that of the Ethiopians. Not only is it filled with wretched twirls, roulades, and ridiculous ornaments, but their chants are of such a length and make their religious ceremonies so exhausting by their dreary monotony that those present have to have crutches under their armpits to be able to stay standing for the duration of the divine service.

The authors of the current report of *Musical Art in Egypt (L'art musical en Egypte)*[132] reproduce a Coptic chant that seems to be in the mode of B. The musical system of the Copts contains ten modes, but the differences between their modulations are so slight and their melody so insipid that the authors cited were in no position to appreciate them.

The Christians of Syria, called JACOBITES, possess no method of notation for their sacred music. What they know of this music is preserved by tradition. They have two kinds of chant as well as two rites, founded respectively by Saint Ephrem, deacon of the church of Edessa, who lived in the year 370, and by a

131. *Musurgia Universalis* (Rome, 1650), vol. 2, pp. 134f.
132. G. A. Villoteau, *De l'état actuel de l'art musical en Egypte* and *Mémoire sur la musique de l'ancien Egypte*, in *Description de l'Egypte*, ed. E. F. Jomar (Paris, 1809–22).

disciple of Eutyches named Jacob. They call the chant of the rite of Saint Ephrem *Meshouhbo Ephremoïto*, and that of the Jacobite rite *Meshouto Jacoboïto*. Each system comprises eight modes, among which one notices the authentic and plagal modulations of the principal Dorian, Phrygian, and Hydean modes, or the Jovian, Martial, and Solar. The Syriac melody is pleasant and far less ornamented than that of the Ethiopians.

The ARMENIANS use a species of accents to notate their music, and these accents do not much differ from the ones they use to indicate their prosodic inflections. But it seems that like the other Oriental peoples, they have come to load their melody, originally very simple, with superfluous ornaments. The proof of this is that Shröder, who published about one hundred years ago a work on the language of the Armenians called *Thesaurus linguae armenicae*, gave the music of the eight tones of the religious chant of these Eastern Christians. Now in his book this music is very simple, whereas in the examples given recently by the French returning from Egypt one finds a host of ornaments that really belong to the taste of the Armenian singer who dictated the songs to them, and which are not expressed in the musical signs that they also recorded.

These Christians attribute the invention of their music to one of the ancient patriarchs who lived about the year 364 and owed it to an inspiration from the Holy Spirit. According to the testimony of those who have been in a position to judge it, this music is one of the best now existing in the East. Its melody depicts the sort of gaiety and happiness enjoyed by naturally active and industrious folk who rejoice in their work and have never known boredom.

The French returning from Egypt, authors of *The*

*Present State of the Musical Art (L'Etat actuel de l'art musical)*[133] in that country, having observed that the Orientals in general have many songs in the form of recitatives, have made very sound reflections on this matter. It is certain, they say, that the ancient Greeks distinguished three types of song: one purely musical, whose tones were modulated; the second, purely oratorical, whose tones were not modulated; the third, participating of both, belonging to poetic recitation. They say that these three kinds of song still exist in Egypt, apart from a few alterations that ignorance and bad taste have forced upon them, but which do not make them so unrecognizable that one cannot still tell them very clearly apart. As much as we take care not to sing when we speak, they say, so much the Ancients were careful to do so; in Egypt all public speeches, sacred or secular, are sung. When the improvising poets or others recite their poetry, they use an instrument to support their voices; this instrument, called *Rebah*, is equipped with a single string, which they use to maintain the key in which they are singing by sustaining the same tone throughout their whole recitation. These reciters, called in Egypt *Mohaddetin*, are veritable rhapsodists who recite the historical or romantic poems of the ancient Arab poets.

Whether in their poetic recitation or in the psalmody they use in their prayers, it is a true musical recitative that can be notated and even supported by an accompaniment.

**France Musicale, 30 July 1843**

133. See previous note.

# XI. DEFINITION OF MELODY; HOW IT IS PRODUCED AND MODIFIED

As COMMONLY DEFINED, melody is a succession of tones so ordered according to the laws of modulation and rhythm that it forms a meaning that pleases the ear. But it seems to me that one might ask those who are content with this definition what they mean by "a meaning that pleases the ear," and how it is possible for a succession of tones to constitute a meaning. I do not believe it has ever been said that painting consists of a succession of colors, nor poetry of a succession of words, although it is evident that their material part consists of nothing else. It is not the succession of tones that makes the melody, but rather the thought that has presided over this succession. Tones which chance or calculation joins together may well offer a pleasant noise to the ear, but not a meaning, just as varied colors may well seduce the eye without presenting anything that resembles a picture.

Let us say it plainly: no melody can exist without a thought, any more than any painting or poem can. Tones, colors, and words are the means that music, painting, or poetry employ to clothe thought in various ways and to give external form to that which previously existed only in the mind. Each of these arts has

137

its appropriate manner of action. Poetry, animated by a general thought, particularizes it to enable it to be grasped; music, on the contrary, struck by a particular thought, generalizes it to increase its beauty and strength. Painting leaves each thought in its own sphere and contents itself with fixing the effect that the other two arts often leave uncertain and fugitive, neither of them being able to dispense with movement, unknown to painting. Thus poetry and music lend each other mutual aid and embellishment; for poetry determines that which in music is too vague, while music expands that which in poetry is too restrained. Thus one can imagine them both as two ministers of thought, of which the first, carrying ideas from heaven to earth, particularizes what is universal, while the second, lifting them up from earth to heaven, universalizes what is particular; whereas painting, fixing the imagination that both poetry and music agitate in opposite directions, holds the soul at the point which it wishes to offer for its contemplation.

After these observations on the nature and the object of music considered as an art, I believe one should define melody, which is its essence, not as a pleasing succession of tones but as the expression of a thought furnished directly or indirectly by poetry and rendered universal from its state of particularity by means of successive tones, whose authenticity, coordination, and length are determined by the laws of the musical system.

As for the thought productive of the melody in particular, or of all that has to do with music or the fine arts in general, here is what the Ancients said of it. They said that genius gives birth to all that is sublime, and that nothing sublime can be born without it, They believed that it belongs to genius alone to speak of divine matters, and that the melody it creates is alone worthy to carry to the gods the prayers of men, and alone capable of awakening in the soul of man the idea and the love of the Divinity. They regarded science as sometimes aiding genius but never replacing it. They attributed to the thought that emanates from it the power of knowing all human affairs and of grasping their relationships. They believed that the melody it creates is fitted to depict the works of Nature, to stir the passions of men or to calm them, to retrace the events of life or to make it happier by lightening toil and solacing pain. The thought of genius presided in the sacred melody, and its true domain was the temple. The thought of science displayed its power in dramatic melody, and ruled principally in the theater.

It was exactly the reverse of what takes place nowadays.

But as it is rare for the soul of man to remain in perfect harmony when the virtue that purifies him is not sufficiently strong to raise him as high as the intellectual light, the Ancients taught that in its perturbation it allows now one faculty to prevail, now another; and that in the event that virtue cedes its empire to vice and grows so feeble as to be on the point of extinction, its principle is obscured, ignorance and systematic pride usurp the place of truth and rule by opinion, prejudice, and self-interest.

When the soul feels only the perturbation of which I have spoken, the thought that emanates from it becomes analogous to whichever of its faculties is dominant. The ideative faculty, exalting the imagination, gives to its productions and particularly to melody a romantic color, and following the part of the soul toward which the psychological principle inclines, creates fantastic objects, depending on reason, passion, or pleasure. The memorative faculty, for its part, acting as sovereign, retraces the memory of the objects by which the soul is most firmly occupied, according to the same laws, and describes them with facility. It is from this that the descriptive faculty emanates, and the theater receives its most striking dramatic scenes, above all when its power is exercised in the irascible and passional part of the soul. Finally, it is from the conceptual faculty that talent largely results: it seizes facilely the relations between things, knows the forms, develops and applies the rules.

The melody it produces is regular but cold, especially when its empire is in sway over the rational part. The passional part warms it a little, but only in the forms. The man whom the ideative faculty guides in his musical compositions has a sort of exaltation that the vulgar may confuse with that of genius, although it differs essentially from it; the man dominated by the memorative faculty has power and charm, and he who follows the conceptual faculty has talent. The first works with fire, the second with spirit, the third with coldness.

One must understand after what I have been saying that one can never teach a person how any melody is made, because it depends entirely on the thought of the composer which takes its rise within his soul, whose character it bears. All one can do is to show to this thought the materials it has to use and the means which Nature has given it of modifying them.

*France Musicale*, 19 February 1843

# XII. Advice to Young Composers concerning Imitation in Music

IT IS SAID of the arts in general and of music in particular that they are the imitation of Nature. This principle is doubtless true if only one knows how to understand it, but however much it may be helpful in this case, it can be equally harmful in the other, that is, when it is not properly understood. Nature, which is the object of imitation in the arts, is certainly not, as the vulgar among artists imagine, the physical nature whose phenomena strike the senses, but that whose marvels manifest themselves to their intelligence. To take as one's sole model the material shapes of the former is to restrict oneself to being nothing but a servile copyist, a cold imitator. It is only through trying to make perceptible the intellectual beauties of the latter that one can pretend to become a creator, and rise to the sublime in any genre whatever. If there is one among the arts to which one can apply the principle in question and say that it is an imitation of Nature, it is indisputably that of painting; however, how mediocre and paltry that painter would be who limited himself to faithfully reproducing on the canvas the form and color of the objects that struck his eyes! His paintings, devoid of sentiment and life, trapped in

the narrow circle of what is called portrait- and genre-
painting, would never rise above caricature. His greatest efforts would only tend to demean the art. He
would imitate Nature exactly, it is true, by copying a
tree, a rock, a flower; by making recognizable at first
glance some person, some animal, or something of the
sort; but this "nature" would certainly not be the one
that inspired Raphael in the composition of his admirable painting of the Transfiguration. Look at those
superb monuments of architecture built to the designs
of Michelangelo or Perrault, and tell me where in physical nature are the models for the Basilica of Saint
Peter or the Colonnade of the Louvre?

The triumph of the arts is not to imitate Nature, as
has been said and thoughtlessly repeated; it is to embellish it and elevate it by giving it what it does not
have, by transporting it beyond its own sphere into a
sphere less circumscribed and more noble. Of all the
arts, music is the one whose triumph of this sort is
the easiest to comprehend; a rigorous imitation of
physical nature not only spoils but annihilates it, so
to speak, by putting in its place something it is not.
A simple experiment will convince one of this truth.

Listen to a capable singer or a skilled player of the
flute or oboe, depicting in the midst of a full orchestra
the warbling of birds; you will be delighted, not in
proportion to the exactitude of the imitation but in
proportion to the sentiments you have once felt, which
the composer's and performer's talents reawaken in
your soul. Nothing is less like the nightingale's song
than these melodic phrases, these harmonic motions
that charm your ears; and yet you recognize what
would have moved you, and you are moved. Now bring
into this orchestra one of those little pipes that children fill with water and twitter with between their

lips, in perfect imitation of the warbling you thought you were hearing; the moment you heard this miserable imitation, all the charm would be destroyed and the pleasure the illusion was giving you would give way to disgust and boredom. This truth has already been perceived and proven: it is quite clear that the animals which are sensitive to music,[134] and children charmed by their nurses' song, look for nothing imitative therein.

The savages repeat their naive or ferocious songs without the intention of imitating anything in Nature. It is from the emotions of their souls that they draw their melody; it is by their accents that they give it expression. The model the composer of music should undertake to imitate is in his own soul. Let him seek and he will find it there, if his soul is susceptible of creating it. If this model is not at his disposal, he will hope in vain to find it anywhere else. What he will draw from material nature will be lifeless, sterile. Not being moved, he will be unable to move others; his most perfect images will be skeletons, and the borrowed finery with which he thinks to clothe their desiccation, if it is merely reminiscence, will always be out of place.

Hear this secret, young composers who are seeking the perfection of the musical art. Know that a correspondence exists between souls, a secret and sympathetic fluid, an unknown electricity that puts them in contact with one another. Of all the means of setting this fluid in motion, music offers the most powerful one. Would you communicate a sentiment, a passion, to your listeners? Would you awaken in them a mem-

---

134. Plutarch, *Symposium*; Buffon, *Histoire naturelle*; Morelet, *De l'expérience musicale*. [FdO]

ory, inspire in them a presentiment? Conceive this sentiment, this passion, strongly; soak yourself in this memory, this presentiment; work! What you have willed shall be. The more energy you have put into feeling, the more strongly you will find your listeners feel. They will experience in their turn, and in proportion to your energy and their own sensibility, the electrical impulse you have imprinted on the sympathetic fluid of which I have spoken. Do not worry about knowing how this works; do not ask me how this impulse can be committed to paper and survive the motive principle that determined it. These metaphysical profundities are not your concern here. Do as I say, if you can, and let it work. But, you will perhaps say, is it sufficient to be soaked in a sentiment in order to communicate it? Is it enough to conceive an idea strongly in order to inspire it? Does one not have to know the necessary means for this? Assuredly one does, and I beg of you not to think otherwise. However great your inspiration, in order to paint you must have brushes, a palette with colors, and know how to use them following the rules of drawing. To want to make music without having become a musician is the height of extravagance and ridicule. Brushes, palette, drawing do not make a painter, but they serve him. Perfect knowledge of musical science, possession of all the melodic and harmonic rules, do not constitute the composer, but without them he can do nothing. The most skillful of flutists cannot demonstrate his talent to me if he does not have the instrument to play on.

Know your art, then; possess all its resources; collect and store up the materials that you need to use; these will be the means for your will to employ in working these wonders. Imagine that from the force of your will, talent will be born, which if directed by genius will know no obstacles. It is genius that will give to the materials of science the life they do not themselves possess; talent will show you how to use them.

Taste will be born from the reaction that you have to the circumstances in which you are placed; for taste is always relative. If, still worrying about the nature of the materials that science furnishes you with, you ask me how you can come to know it, and in what way you can, for example, distinguish the means of giving to melody a character of sadness or gaiety, tenderness and strength, I will answer that this will depend precisely on the rightness of your sentiment and on the force of will that you use for expressing it. If, wishing to depict sorrow, you can immerse yourself in this sentiment, the means you will need to characterize it will arrive of themselves and be put to work by your will according to the extent of your talent. It is the same for gaiety and the other moral affections. Images will be no more difficult. The pictures you create will always depend on the aptitude you have for grasping and representing them to yourself. If you lack the direct means to express your ideas, if you suffer this kind of poverty that always comes from a lack of science, you will see that your will goes to gather all possible indirect means to supply it; and often you will be very surprised to see that the very things that in other circumstances passed for representing sorrow have lent themselves to the depiction of pleasure.

*France Musicale*, 17 November 1844

**XIIa.** Feel strongly what you want to make felt. I assure you, there is no other principle of musical ex-

pression. It is the only way to attain it, for composer
and performer alike. The primary inspiration belongs
to one, the secondary conception to the other; one
determines the cause, the other propagates the effect.
When a piece of vocal or instrumental music is well
composed, that is to say when it harbors in itself the
expression of whatever sentiment emanated from
the composer, it is very rare for the artist entrusted
with its performance not to feel it, however slight his
gift. This is the very touchstone of the executant's
talent.

You may be certain that if an instrumentalist or a
singer, having before him a piece of music in which
the composer has really placed an affection of the soul,
cannot distinguish it, then he lacks this affection himself; and if this happens to him frequently and in many
different circumstances, say bluntly that there is a
poverty of soul here, a want of moral resource that
will always prevent him from being a distinguished
artist.

It is by examining attentively and with proper reflection the music composed by the great masters and
unanimously accepted by performers as containing the
expression of a certain sentiment, that you will learn
to know the positive means that science offers you to
express your thought. You will find these means even
more simply and accessibly in folk song, in national
songs, in the precious remnants of ancient music; but
you are quite wrong if you think that these means, to
whatever degree of perfection you possess them, can
take the place of sentiment in yourself and make an
effect outside you, if you have never developed its
cause within you. Know once again that there is no
effect without a cause, that nothing can come of noth-

ing, and that one hopes in vain to find in anything what one has not put into it.

It has sometimes been said that music is a universal language. That is true in one sense. One can in fact communicate by means of music the sentiments, the affections, even the emotions; what one must note well is that this communication always works in a general way and without particularizing anything.

Music, altogether intellectual in its essence, cannot receive physical forms except by means of poetry.

Without the help of poetry which fixes its ideas, it would always remain vague and indeterminate. This is why these two sciences were never separated in Antiquity. They even added to them that of the dance, that is, the kind of art that under the name of mime regulated the movements of the body and presided over what we call declamation and gesture. It is certain that a perfect music can never exist without the union of these three things: the word that determines the idea, the melody that communicates to it the sentiment, and the rhythmic movement that characterizes its expression. It is also true to say that music separated from poetry and become purely instrumental is far from enjoying all its advantages: it is a kind of soul deprived of a body that falls into vaguenesses and lacks the means to make its beauties felt. If dance properly so called does not sustain it, it will not long avoid the boredom that always accompanies to some degree the indecision of the spirit. The perfection of the performance may for a moment provoke curiosity and hold the attention, but attention soon tires, and curiosity, which must be stimulated more and more, is blunted and falls asleep. Composers and instrumentalists then make efforts to awaken it, but their *tours de force,* their bizarre efforts of every kind only end by disgusting it altogether. Then one must return to poetry.[135] Follow the advice I have given: do not separate, if you can avoid it, three sisters who love each other ardently and who embellish one another. Cultivate poetry, music, and declamation, and if circumstances compel you to work for instruments alone, begin at least by studying the effects of your art on the melodies where poetry has left its indelible traces. It is by this means alone that you will educate yourself to melody and have a musical style that is your own. Let those who want to, fumble on an instrument to find motives of melody that poetry refuses them: these motives, which nothing determines, will last as long as the caprice that gave them birth.

Read much ancient music, go through the works of the great composers, study the poets, go to hear good declaimers.

Seek, labor, do not weary.

*France Musicale*, 24 November 1844

---

135. The text of this sentence reads: "Il faut alors revenir à la poésie, et la simplicité abandonnée, venait de l'abus même qu'on avait fait des ornements," to which Pinasseau adds a note: "Texte incomplet, conforme à celui de la revue."

# APPENDIXES

# A. Harmony among the Greeks and Romans[136]

The loss of that essential part of music known as harmony must be attributed to the numerous revolutions of which our hemisphere has been the stage, and to the darkness that has long veiled the face of the earth. We are convinced that in ancient times India as well as China knew its most secret elements, while Greece and even Rome were not ignorant of it. To be persuaded of this truth in relation to Greece and Rome, it is enough to open the books that speak either directly or indirectly of music. Plato seems to allude to it in several places,[137] but where he leaves us in no doubt whatever is in the *Laws*, when after censuring the abuse that musicians have made of it, he exclaims:

"If the Muses were inspiring these composers, they would not outrage truth to the point of adapting to

136. This article appeared again in *La France Musicale* on 11 August 1850, under the title: "Si les anciens ont connu l'harmonie?" ["Did the Ancients know of harmony?"], under the signature F. D., with the following variants: the article begins "Everything indicates to me that . . ."; in paragraph 1, sentence 2 begins "I am persuaded that . . ."; at the end of paragraph 3, adds: "This philosopher absolutely does not want children to waste their time in getting adept at it, and here he gives another unequivocal proof of the existence of harmony." The notes to works cited are not in the article as it appeared in 1850. [JP]

137. *Philosophus, Laches, Theatetus.* [FdO]

words that are masculine and full of nobility an effeminate and feeble melody. . . . They would not mingle the cries of animals and endless roulades with human and instrumental voices, nor give this confusion of all sorts of sounds for simple imitation. It is only musicians without inspiration who could confuse and mix up all these things without taste and without principles. They deserve to be the laughingstock of those who, as Orpheus says, have received a share in the graces of harmony."[138]

After having spoken thus strongly against the abuse of harmony, Plato attacks, a little further on, that of proliferating instrumental difficulties and *tours de force* in playing the lute and the flute. He laughs at the frivolous roulades that were played extremely fast, without missing a note, and regards them as the effect of gross ignorance and vain ostentation:

"With respect to this disparity and variety of tones, when one plays one part on the lyre while the singer performs another, and when by opposing frequent and infrequent tones, fast and slow ones, high or low, one makes a chord out of discord itself; also with respect to the rhythms that are infinitely varied by accommodating them to the notes of the lyre, it is unnecessary to have children practice all these fine points of the art."[139]

The Greeks were not the only ones to know simple harmony and to apply, it, as we have seen, but they also used a sort of figured harmony by means of which they composed in three modes at once. Sacadas and Clonas won their fame in these sorts of difficult com-

138. *Laws*, II, [669]. [FdO]
139. *Laws*, VII, [812]. This passage is peremptory, and one cannot see after reading it how anyone can have doubted that the Greeks knew harmony and instrumental accompaniment. [FdO]

positions. Stratonicus also passed as having invented certain chords, along with the method of notating them.[140]

The Romans, in receiving melody from the Greeks, received their harmony as well. Seneca makes it clear enough in this passage, which allows of no ambiguity:

"Do you not see how many different voices a choir is composed of? Yet from all these diverse tones there results but a single one. There are high, low, and middle voices; male and female voices unite, the flutes mingle in their tones, yet all this is heard simultaneously without anything in particular dominating. . . . In our theaters there are more musicians than spectators. . . . Nevertheless, although all the passages are filled with singers, the amphitheater lined with trumpets and all sorts of other instruments, from so many different tones there arises only a general chord."[141]

One would assuredly have to be as stubborn as could be to refuse to see harmony there. The Greeks knew it without a doubt; but from Plato's century on, it was already tending to corruption among them. The Romans, who did not know its principles, carried its abuse to excess; soon it disappeared along with the very body of music in the thick of the political storms that overturned the Empire, scattered its debris, and buried it under torrents of filth. Perhaps some frail remnants floated up with the fragment of melody that survived these disasters, but, to tell the truth, the fanaticism of the first Christians was opposed to this, since they regarded it, together with all the beautiful sciences, as inspirations of the infernal spirit and as

140. Athenaeus, I, viii, ch. 2. [FdO]
141. *Epistle* 84. [FdO]

impious creations that must be stifled to the root. Several Fathers of the Church persecuted them relentlessly. Without the efforts of Pope Gregory I, perhaps some writings on the nature of Greek and Roman harmony would have reached us; but he did not permit anything that had survived the barbarian sword to escape the flames of his bonfires. One proof that the destruction of harmony was truly in the spirit of Christianity is that at the epoch of Luther's Reformation, when there was question of restoring the Church to its ancient purity, that is, to the somber and superstitious rigidity from which the culture of arts and letters had begun to remove it, Calvin,[142] the fiercest of the Reformers, did not fail to prohibit music as an infernal invention, and was the reason that games and shows were prohibited in Geneva, and that for a hundred years no musical instrument was seen in that town.

For the rest, this remark had not escaped the sagacity of certain modern writers who, studying the history of music without religious prejudices, saw clearly that the loss of this science was not attributable to the barbarians alone. One of them, noticing the host of contradictions in the writers of the first fifteen centuries of our era, expressed himself thus on the subject:

"A more intelligent and powerful will controlled the pens of the writers of that time: it dictated to them the most absurd and inconsequential ideas, which it then had the authorities adopt, or else it hid them under specious and almost inextricable sophistries. Those who instituted or simplified the art of notation did not lack musical intelligence, but a monastic

---

142. The same remarks in *Histoire philosophique du genre humain* (1979), vol. II, p. 195 (English translation, pp. 371f.), where Calvin is contrasted with his fellow Genevan J.-J. Rousseau.

Machiavellianism made them bury it, and substituted an incomplete system that would consign ancient music to oblivion, and especially the beautiful songs of Greece . . ."[143] He adds a little later: "The musical style had been mutilated not by the invasion of Europe by the barbarians, as we have often heard tell, but in fact by the prejudices of a religious cult that was easily persuaded that it was in its own interest to stifle not only the memories of the beautiful songs of Greece, but even to remove the means of composing similar ones by overthrowing all the principles of music."[144]

**"An Antiquary"**
***France Musicale*, 30 June 1844**

143. [P.-J. J. de la Salette,] *Considérations sur les [divers] systèmes de la musique [ancienne et moderne, et sur le genre enharmonique des Grecs* (Paris, 1810)], vol. II, p. 79. [FdO]
144. Op. cit., vol. II, p. 104. [FdO]

# B. THE ORIGIN OF NOTATION AND OF MODERN MUSIC

IT SEEMS very difficult for us today to say why Pope Gregory, wishing to discard two modes from his system in order to deliver them to the entertainments of the multitude, chose precisely those of C and A. It would be equally difficult to know exactly the reasons that made him suppress the *hypate-hypaton* string, B. One might suspect that whatever form his ideas took, they are fundamentally not much different from those of Saint Ambrose, when that bishop mixed up the names of the modes and confused them with one another. Their common intent was always to denature the Greek system and cause it to be forgotten. Their success in this regard was at first complete: for more than ten centuries people used only their modes. Secular music, regarded as sacrilegious, was banned; the very modes that they had allowed to the lay public were abandoned so utterly that it would be hard to find a single vestige of them. It was only toward the beginning of the eleventh century that Guido d'Arezzo dared to make a few attempts at them, always excusing himself and protesting that he had certainly not followed the procedure of the philosophers in his exposition of musical rules, but that he stuck strictly to what was necessary for the Church's use and for the education of children.

This Guido d'Arezzo, also known as Guy Aretino, justly celebrated by modern musicians, rendered two very important services to the sciences: first, by inventing or perfecting the dots that serve today as musical notes; second, by giving names to these notes. By the first he facilitated the rebirth of harmony and gave it new developments; by the second, he made melody easier to retain and to learn. Harmony was at first called "counter-point" because of the dots that notated it, placed above or below one another. Even in its feeble state it displeased the Sacred College; thus we see in 1316 Pope John XXII declare by Papal Bull[145] that he did not permit the newly invented chords to be mixed in with the Church's chants, lest the counterpoint should stifle the noble simplicity of the chants then in use. The secular power itself was no more indulgent, for despite the permission that Louis IX had given for the formation of an Academy of Music, the Parliament of Paris closed it on the pretext that the musicians did not confine themselves to following the ecclesiastical rules and moved too frequently from one genus and one mode to another.

As for the names that Guido d'Arezzo gave to the notes, formed as everyone knows from the first syllables of the lines of a hymn to Saint John, one should note that he restricted himself to the first six, Ut, Re, Mi, Fa, Sol, La, not daring to name Sa, the seventh, as he could have done and doubtless would, if orders from above had not prevented him. One surprising thing that cannot be the result of pure chance is that this essential note went nearly five centuries without a

145. The Bull was issued in 1324/5 at Avignon.

name, while all the others had names, despite the awkwardness that this caused and the difficulty of saying Mi Fa when it would have been simple to say Si Ut. It was only about the year 1650 that this syllable Sa or Si was introduced into the scale where it was so badly needed. Furetière says that a musician named Lemaître proposed it for thirty years,[146] but met with such difficulties that he died without having succeeded in getting it accepted, and that it was only after his death that it finally triumphed over the vocal opposition of a few old conservatives. The writer to whom I owe this anecdote, seeing such a simple thing meet with so many obstacles, could not prevent himself from thinking that there must have been some great interest opposing its adoption. That was certainly so, and one might suspect, now that one knows the influence of this note on the musical system, how important it was to conceal it. For the rest, it was definitely not the musicians who were at fault in this case, because they had to respect the laws that they had been given; it was for the highest priestly authority, having established these laws in an age of darkness, to consider whether the time had come to modify them. If this authority had known how to profit from the incipient dawn it would not have set itself in opposition to it, nor exposed the virtue of musicians in a fight against reason and even against authority. But this supreme priesthood saw fit to remain in the dark while the people became enlightened.

What happened, then? That which naturally had to

146. Antoine Furetière, author of *Dictionnaire universel* (1690); Jean Lemaire [sic], cited in Marin Mersenne, *Harmonie universelle* (1632), *Traité des consonnances*, bk. VI, p. 342, as the inventor of a new notational system. See *New Grove Dictionary of Music and Musicians*, s.v. "Lemaire."

happen. Sacred music, whose shortcomings were daily being laid bare and to which no beauty was being added, was abandoned, and secular music, escaping at last from its chains, waxed strong, gathered all the votes, and overwhelmed its feeble rival.

It was rhythm, entirely unknown to the older music, that contributed most to the success of this one as it was introduced under the name of meter. Jean de Muris[147] was the author of this admirable invention which gave to each tone a relative duration, representing it by means of certain signs affixed to the noteheads. He was bold enough to be the first to conceive of rhythm abstractly and to apply it to the music in isolation, independently of the syllabic plod of language. This idea, very fortunate in itself and expressed in a manner both clear and easy, made the greatest contribution in these modern times to the perfection of the art. The Ancients had doubtless known musical rhythm, and the Troubadours surely introduced a kind of meter into their music; but none of them discovered the means, apparently so simple yet in fact so difficult, of determining this rhythm or this meter in such a way as to present it to the mind, as it were drawing it on the paper even to the finest nuances of movement. This invention, justly called admirable, must give our music an incontestable superiority over that of all other peoples without exception — so long as its system, founded on true principles, uses only the correct tunings.

Meanwhile, the inventions of Guido d'Arezzo and Jean de Muris had given a great impulse to the common man's music. Soon the notes of the system were expanded to cover four octaves, and finally they dis-

147. Author of *Ars novae musicae* (1319).

covered the ascending chromatic genus, by means of the sharp that they used as a musical symbol (the flat being already in use as the sign of the descending chromatic genus). Harmony, as distinct from counterpoint, came to perfection, and Italy, Spain, and France were filled with theaters in which dramatic music very soon made extremely rapid progress.

**F.D.\*\*\*.**
*France Musicale*, 1 August 1852

# c. The Music of the Phoenicians

THE MUSIC of the Phoenicians, according to Fabre d'Olivet who is our guide in this historical work, was divided into as many branches and formed as many individual systems as there were sects among them. These different sects which gave their names to the peoples among whom they dominated also served to designate the types of music they favored. Hence came the Lydian mode (the mode of Venus or of the universal generative faculty), the Phrygian (that of the chief or the shepherd-king), the Dorian (that of liberty or the masculine energy), the Ionian (that of the dove or the feminine nature), etc. Each of the different modes found among the Greeks had its own character. Of all of them, the one that seems to have been the most generally adopted in Phoenicia was the mode popularly called "common," which the Greeks knew under the name Locrian, signifying the characteristic mode of alliance. The fundamental string of this mode was A, which dominated in the Phoenician musical system first at high pitch, then even at low pitch when it was added there. As this string was assimilated to the Moon, which held first rank among the divinities of the Amazonian peoples (devotees, that is, of the feminine nature), they gave to its mode the name *lyn*, meaning star of the night, and after the custom of those times made it into a mythical personage who, subsequently passing for a famous musician, was cited as the singing-master of Hercules. However, Herodotus states formally that it was a sort of song used in Egypt that had passed from the bosom of Phoenicia into Europe.[148] This sort of song that he calls *linos* was, he says, of a sad and melancholic character. This corresponds precisely to the idea that the modern Chinese still have of this Phoenician mode, whose tonic, A, they designate by the expressive epithet *housi*, "Western lamentation."

At the moment when the Shepherds dismembered the Indian Empire and formed the famous sect that gave birth to the Phoenician nation,[149] it seems that they chose to designate the seven diatonic tones of their musical system by the seven vowels of their alphabet, in such a way that the first of these vowels, *alpha* or A, was applied to the Cyprian principle F, which they regarded as first, and the last, *ain*, which the Greeks rendered by *omega* and we by *ou*, was applied to the Saturnian principle B, which they considered as the last. One may believe that it was as a natural consequence of this way of notating the two musical strings, assimilated to the two principles of the Universe, that was born the famous proverb put in the mouth of the Supreme Being to designate his omnipotence and immensity:

## "I AM THE ALPHA AND THE OMEGA"[150]

148. See note 22.
149. See note 114.
150. Revelation 1:8, 21:6, 22:13.

However, either because the Phoenicians had two methods of notating the tones, or whether they considered them as proceeding by harmonic intervals, B, E, A, D, G, C, F, or by diatonic ones, B, C, D, E, F, G, A; or because time or political and religious revolutions caused certain changes in their notation, it is clear from several passages in ancient writers that the A string, assimilated to the Moon and the tonic of the *common* or Locrian mode, was notated by the vowel A; so that the entire scale sung from high to low was solfèged to the seven Phoenician vowels, unknown today; and in going from high to low it went consequently from right to left, instead of from low to high and from left to right. The Shepherds, in breaking away from the Indian Empire, adopted this method which they passed on to those who depended directly or indirectly on them. The Egyptians, the Arabs, the Assyrians, the Greeks, the Etruscans received it and conserved it for a longer or shorter time according to circumstances. The Arabs and all those who received the yoke of Islam still follow it to this day.

**Escudier, *Dictionnaire de Musique***

# D. THE MUSIC OF THE EGYPTIANS

IF WE are to believe certain writers whose evidence deserves serious consideration, the Egyptians borrowed their musical system from the Phoenicians. One can deduce this fact from a tablet of Demetrius Phalerus, whence it is certain that the seven vowels of the Oriental languages served these peoples as musical characters and even as tones for solfège.[151] Inscriptions found in Egypt and Phoenicia contain musical invocations addressed to the seven planets. Each planet is designated by a word composed of seven vowels, beginning with the vowel consecrated to the planet invoked. These invocations, which comprise the seven diatonic modes, are very valuable since they prove the existence of these modes and their application in the remotest antiquity.

The priests of Egypt, says an ancient author, sang to the gods by sounding the seven vowels. For them, this sound replaced by its harmony that of the flute and the lyre.

151. Compare *La Langue hébraïque restituée*, Ch. II, sect. 1 (English translation, pp. 73f.). Fabre d'Olivet's authority on this subject was probably J. J. Barthélémy, in his *Remarques sur les medailles d'Antonin, frappées en Egypte*, and *Lettre à M. de Cabanon*, in his *Oeuvres Complètes*, 1831. (Cited in Edmond Bailly, *Le Chant des voyelles* [Paris, 1911], p. 33.)

Even when the Egyptians shook off the yoke of the Shepherd Kings, they do not seem to have given up this way of writing and singing music. We know that this people had the greatest aversion to novelties of any sort. Even the changes introduced in the government exercised only a slight influence on the form of the musical system. The people were used to certain songs which it would have been dangerous to try to take away from them.

The Phoenician mode called *lyn* was much used in Egypt under the name *maneh*, an epithet given to the Moon, on account of the month that this heavenly body measures in its course. Athenaeus reports that they used to accompany nuptial songs with an instrument called *mon-aule*, that is, in Egyptian, a flute in the *monet* or lunar mode.

Moreover, the Egyptian priests preserved the memory of the civil troubles that after ravaging the earth had caused their country's long enslavement, and prudence guided them in not leaving to the mercy of the people that knowledge which could be made evil use of. Thus they buried in the secrecy of the sanctuary the principles of all the sciences, displaying only visible symbols, ingenious enough to pique the curiosity but never clear enough to be understood except in long meditations and through initiations that were progressively more difficult to obtain.

Thus the principles of music, like those of all the other sciences, were carefully enshrined in the sanctuaries of Egypt. It was there that Orpheus learned them, and that Pythagoras was worthy to receive them after Orpheus.

A few fragments of music have come down to us that are presumed to have belonged to the Egyptians. There is one in particular that the learned Burette has deciphered from the Greek notation. He attributes its words to a certain poet named Dionysius Iambos,[152] who was practically a contemporary of Aristotle. But one cannot suppose that such an obscure poet could have composed so beautiful a melody, which corresponds so well to the idea that the Ancients have given us of the sacred songs of Egypt.

This ancient fragment is in the solar mode; that is to say, its natural tonic is the E string.

As we have seen above, Orpheus and Pythagoras borrowed the musical system of Egypt and enriched it with numerous improvements (see on this subject the article "Greece").[153]

## Escudier, *Dictionnaire de Musique*[154]

152. Greek poet, fourth century B.C.E., mentioned by Suidas, Plutarch (*De Musica* 15), and Clement of Alexandria.
153. I.e., Chapter IX of this book, "The Musical System of the Greeks."
154. I translate directly from the first edition (1844); Pinasseau's text is from some later, abbreviated edition.

# E. BRIEF EXPOSITION
# OF THE MUSICAL SYSTEM[155]

EVERY TONE that sounds can be conceived under the
form of unity. Every tone includes all tones. But the
string that gives it can be divided into parts, and from
the moment it is divided, it produces other tones that
are analogous to the generating tone, but whose analogy is harmonic or inharmonic. For the notes produced
to be harmonic, the division of the string must be
made according to geometrical proportions. The quaternary of Pythagoras 1, 2, 3, 4, supplies the only proportions admissible in music. These proportions are
remarkable in that they proceed according to an arith-
metical and geometrical progression. Every other progression than that contained or produced by the quaternary 1, 2, 3, 4, gives only tones that are inharmonic,
false, and heterogeneous.

A string conceived in its unity gives a certain tone
which acquires its properties and a name only from
the relation it has with other tones. A tone must necessarily be considered as producer or product. But a

155. From *La Vraie Maçonnerie et la Céleste Culture*, manuscript published with introduction and notes by Léon Cellier (Grenoble, 1953; reprinted Lausanne: La Proue, 1973), pp. 69–71.

tone can only produce other tones through the division one makes in the string which gives it; and it can be produced only by means of the division one has made of a generating string to which it belongs.

Let us then take a string as producer, and begin by submitting it to the quaternary progression 1, 2, 3, 4. We will call this string B. Divided from 1 into 2, it will give its own octave and not depart from its diapason: thus we will have done nothing for the musical system, for B is no different from B. And however much one may raise or lower this B from octave to octave, it will never produce any melody. This proves that the two principial principles 1 and 2 cannot act in their essence. They can only act in their faculty. Now the faculty of 1 is imparity (oddness), and the faculty of 2 is parity (evenness). The number 3, being the first number, thus displays the faculty of 1; and consequently 4 displays the faculty of 2, whose power it is. But if a string be divided in 3, it cannot be divided in 4; for evenness and oddness are incompatible. So we need two strings, the one to represent the principle 1, which we shall divide into 3; the other to represent the principle 2, which we shall divide into 4. But what are these strings which we are to divide thus? They must necessarily be those strings which in producing themselves reciprocally, produce reciprocally all the other tones, without exceeding the musical septenary given by Nature. Now the two strings that fulfill these conditions are F and B. These strings form between them an irrational and incommensurable interval. They are opposed to one another as even is to odd. So let the F string be divided into 3, representing the principial principle 1. This string thus divided produces its fifth C by proceeding from 3 to 2. Next let the B string be divided by 4, representing the principial

THE SECRET LORE OF MUSIC

principle 2. This string thus divided produces its fifth E by proceeding from 4 to 3. By continuing the progression from 3 to 2 for the string F, it develops from fifth to fifth: F, C, G, D, A, E, B. In continuing the progression of 4 to 3 for the B string, it develops from fourth to fourth: B, E, A, D, G, C, F. Thus these two strings mutually produce each other by opposite paths; and in so doing they give birth to all the notes of the scale. One should observe that the note on which the two strings meet is D. The note D is thus the archetype of unison. It represents Mars in the planetary system. This system is conceived starting from the B string as follows:

| B | E | A | D | G | C | F |
|---|---|---|---|---|---|---|
| Saturn | Sun | Moon | Mars | Mercury | Jupiter | Venus |
| Saturday | Sunday | Monday | Tuesday | Wednesday | Thursday | Friday |

In conceiving this system in the diatonic order, one obtains:

| B | C | D | E | F | G | A |
|---|---|---|---|---|---|---|
| Saturn | Jupiter | Mars | Sun | Venus | Mercury | Moon |

Thus the Sun is at the center of the Universe, a fourth distant from Saturn and a fourth from the Moon. But the string that gives the fourth from Saturn to the Moon is far shorter than that which gives the fourth from Saturn to the Sun.

If one continues the progression of the F string from 3 to 2 it produces the sharp and destroys itself by the action of the B string of which the sharp is the direct production and latent principle.[156] B produced by F represents Love or the expansive Force; F produced by B represents Chaos or the compressive Force: the primordial principles of the Universe. These musical notions are sufficient for theory.

156. That is, if one continues the progression from F beyond B, the next term is F sharp, a nondiatonic tone.

# F. The Schism
# in the Universal Empire[157]

I HAVE INDICATED in another work[158] the singular cause that came to trouble the harmony that reigned in the greatest and finest empire ever seen on earth before or since; and I entered there into very extensive details that will not be allowed here. This cause — who would believe it? — had its feeble beginnings in music. To understand this, we must take leave for a moment of the prejudices of our youth, and understand well what Pythagoras, Zoroaster, Khung Fu-tzu, Plato, and all the sages of Antiquity said: that music is the universal science: the science without which one cannot penetrate the inner essence of anything. This science, however, was here only the pretext for the collapse that occurred. Its true cause was the nature of man, which, ever driving him ahead in his course, cannot for a moment leave him stationary in a single place. His intelligence once stirred cannot rest; a profound truth moves him even unconsciously; he feels

157. From *Histoire philosophique du genre humain*, vol. I, pp. 244–46 (English translation, pp. 147–50).
158. Presumably the present book is meant. The idea was first mentioned by Fabre d'Olivet in *Les Vers Dorés de Pythagore expliqués*, 1813 ed., p. 25.

that he is not in his proper place, and that he must get there. Intellectual men soon become contemplatives: they want to know the reason for everything; and, as the Universe is linked to their exploration, one feels that they have much to do, and many an opportunity for self-deceit.

I have already said that at the epoch when the Celts conquered the Indies, they found established there a complete system of metaphysical and physical sciences. It seems certain that at that time the Atlantean cosmology all referred to absolute Unity, and made everything emanate from and depend on a single principle. This unique principle, called *Ishvara*, was conceived as purely spiritual. One cannot deny that this doctrine has great advantages; but one must also agree that it involves certain difficulties, above all when the people to whom it is given are not in the right circumstances for its reception. In order for the doctrine of absolute Unity to remain purely spiritual, and not to lead the people whose religion it is into abject materialism and anthropomorphism, it is necessary for this people to be enlightened enough always to reason correctly — or unenlightened enough never to reason at all. If it has only a half-enlightened intellect, and if its physical knowledge leads it to draw correct conclusions from certain principles whose falsity it cannot see, its deviation is inevitable; it will either become atheist, or change the dogma.

Since it is proved that the Atlanteans accepted the dogma of a single principle, and that this principle was up to then in harmony with their situation, one cannot refuse to believe that they had reached the highest degree of the social state. Their empire had embraced the earth; but doubtless after having shed their brightest beams, their lights began to grow dim when the

Celts conquered them. The Hindus, who succeeded them in another part of the earth, although they were their most educated disciples, were far from possessing the same powers. Their government still worked, thanks to the impulse it had received; but already their resources were depleted, and the life-principles that animated it no longer renewed themselves.

Such was the state of affairs even several centuries before the arrival of Ram. It is evident that if this Theocrat had not found the empire of the Atlanteans in decline and tottering on its foundations, he would not only have found it less easy to appropriate it — he would not even have attempted to do so; for Providence would not have determined him for it. As I said, he adopted the divine Unity, to which he added the cult of the Ancestors; and finding all the sciences founded on a unique principle, he gave them thus to his peoples to study.

But it happened after a longer or shorter interval that one of the sovereign Pontiffs, examining the musical system of Bharata that was believed to be founded upon a single principle like all the rest, noticed that it was not so, and that it was necessary to admit two principles for the generation of tones.[159]

Now, what made music such an important science for the Ancients was the faculty they recognized therein of serving as an easy passage from the physical to the intellectual; so that by transferring the ideas that it furnished from one nature to the other, they thought themselves authorized to pronounce by analogy, proceeding from the known to the unknown. In

159. I have gone into this subject in great detail, as also into those that I have only indicated here, in a work on Music which will very shortly be published. [FdO]

their hands, music was thus a kind of proportional measure that they applied to spiritual essences.

When the discovery that this sovereign Pontiff had made in the musical system was divulged and known throughout the Empire, the contemplative scholars did not hesitate to seize on it and to use it, as was their practice, to explain the cosmogonic laws of the Universe; and soon they were astonished to see that what they had hithero considered as the product of an absolute Unity was that of a combined Duality. Doubtless they could have been undismayed by this idea, and have put everything back in place by regarding the two principles whose existence they had been forced to recognize as primordial, rather than regarding them as principial,[160] just as the first Zoroaster would do some centuries later; but for this they would have had to raise themselves to heights which their intelligence could not yet attain. Accustomed to see all things in Ishvara, they lacked the courage to dispossess him of his supremacy, and preferred to duplicate him, so to speak, by joining to him a new principle that they called *Prakriti*, that is to say, Nature. This new principle possessed the *shakti* or the conceptive power, and the former Ishvara the *bidja*, the generative and vivifying power.

The result of this first step, which took a considerable time, was thus to consider the Universe as the product of two principles, each possessing as its particularity either the male or the female faculty. This system, whose simplicity was at first attractive, was generally adopted. Among most peoples one finds these two Principles invoked under a multitude of names.

160. Fabre uses the terms *principiés* and *principiants*, literally "principiated" and "principiating."

# INDEX